Grupo Clarín

From its emergence as a modest newspaper to becoming the largest communication group in Argentina, and one of the main communications groups in Latin America, this book examines the media conglomerate Grupo Clarín.

Guillermo Mastrini, Martín Becerra and Ana Bizberge analyze the group's corporate structure and the aspects that have contributed to its expansion throughout its history, mapping its stages of growth to the regulatory policies, cultural politics, economics and political history of Argentina over the last few decades. This book offers a compelling analysis of one of the key players in the Latin American communication and information market, highlighting how the conglomerate has continued to grow under various different governments – by achieving legal reforms and influencing policies – and continues to have great capacity to influence the policy and regulation of the system, the market structure and cultural consumption in the region.

This book is ideal for students, scholars and researchers of global media, political economy, and media and communication, especially those with an interest in Latin America.

Guillermo Mastrini is a Professor at Universidad Nacional de Quilmes and Universidad de Buenos Aires. He is also member of CONICET, Argentina. He is co-editor of *Political Economy, Communication and Knowledge: A Latin American Perspective* (2012). He has been consultant for UNESCO, the Friedrich Ebert Foundation and Open Society Foundations. He is member of the board of OBSERVACOM.

Martín Becerra is a Professor at Universidad Nacional de Quilmes and Universidad de Buenos Aires. He is also member of the Consejo Nacional de Investigaciones Científicas y Tecnológicas, Argentina. He has been consultant for UNESCO, Amnesty International, Reporters Without Borders, the Swedish International Cooperation Agency, the Friedrich Ebert Foundation and Open Society Foundations.

Ana Bizberge is the Head of the MA in Cultural Industries at Universidad Nacional de Quilmes and she is a professor at Universidad de Buenos Aires, Universidad de San Martín and Universidad Torcuato Di Tella, where she teaches media policy and economics and communication theories. She is also content editor at OBSERVACOM.

Global Media Giants
Series editors: Benjamin J. Birkinbine, Rodrigo Gomez and Janet Wasko

Since the second half of the 20th century, the significance of media corporate power has been increasing in different and complex ways around the world; the power of these companies in political, symbolic and economic terms has been a global issue and concern. In the 21st century, understanding media corporations is essential to understanding the political, economic and socio-cultural dimensions of our contemporary societies.

The **Global Media Giants** series continues the work that began in the series editors' book *Global Media Giants*, providing detailed examinations of the largest and most powerful media corporations in the world.

Tencent
The Political Economy of China's Surging Internet Giant
Min Tang

Grupo Prisa
Media Power in Contemporary Spain
Luis A. Albornoz, Ana I. Segovia, and Núria Almiron

Amazon
Understanding a Global Communication Giant
Benedetta Brevini and Lukasz Swiatek

Grupo Clarín
From Argentine Newspaper to Convergent Media Conglomerate
Guillermo Mastrini, Martín Becerra, and Ana Bizberge

For more information about this series, please visit: https://www.routledge.com/Global-Media-Giants/book-series/GMG

Grupo Clarín
From Argentine Newspaper to Convergent Media Conglomerate

**Guillermo Mastrini
Martín Becerra, and
Ana Bizberge**

TRANSLATION AND EDITING OF ENGLISH VERSION:
MARITA PROPATO.

TRANSLATION TEAM: LAURA ESTEFANÍA,
MELISSA POLITE, CAMILA CARNEVALE,
AND MARÍA LÁZARA.

NEW YORK AND LONDON

First published 2021
by Routledge
605 Third Avenue, New York, NY 10158

and by Routledge
2 Park Square, Milton Park, Abingdon, Oxon, OX14 4RN

Routledge is an imprint of the Taylor & Francis Group, an informa business

© 2021 Taylor & Francis

The right of Guillermo Mastrini, Martín Becerra, and Ana Bizberge to be identified as authors of this work has been asserted by them in accordance with sections 77 and 78 of the Copyright, Designs and Patents Act 1988.

All rights reserved. No part of this book may be reprinted or reproduced or utilised in any form or by any electronic, mechanical, or other means, now known or hereafter invented, including photocopying and recording, or in any information storage or retrieval system, without permission in writing from the publishers.

Trademark notice: Product or corporate names may be trademarks or registered trademarks, and are used only for identification and explanation without intent to infringe.

Library of Congress Cataloging-in-Publication Data
Names: Mastrini, Guillermo, author. | Becerra, Martín, 1968– author. | Bizberge, Ana, author.
Title: Grupo Clarín : from Argentine newspaper to convergent media conglomerate / Guillermo Mastrini, Martín Becerra, and Ana Bizberge.
Description: New York : Routledge, 2021. | Series: Global media giants | Includes bibliographical references and index.
Subjects: LCSH: Clarín (Firm)—History. | Conglomerate corporations—Argentina—History. | Mass media policy—Argentina. | Mass media—Law and legislation—Argentina. | Communication policy—Argentina. | Communication policy—Latin America. | Organizational change—Argentina.
Classification: LCC HD2830.12.G78 M37 2021 (print) | LCC HD2830.12.G78 (ebook) | DDC 338.7/61302230982—dc23
LC record available at https://lccn.loc.gov/2021011652
LC ebook record available at https://lccn.loc.gov/2021011653

ISBN: 978-0-367-50734-3 (hbk)
ISBN: 978-0-367-50736-7 (pbk)
ISBN: 978-1-003-05106-0 (ebk)

Typeset in Times New Roman
by codeMantra

Contents

List of Figures   vii
List of Tables   ix

Introduction   1

1 Understanding *Clarín*: An Overview of Argentine History   7
Introduction 7
1945–1955. Peronism, the Media and Clarín *8*
Cycle of Political Unrest 10
*The Dictatorship and the Media: Control
   and Privatization 14*
*The Return to Democracy: Alfonsín,
   Menem and De la Rúa 16*
Kirchnerism 21
Recent Years 25
Notes 26
References 26

2 Politics under the Skin   28
A Wake-Up Call (1945–1958) 28
The Developmentalist Platform (1958–1976) 31
Dictatorship and Deals (1976–1983) 34
Democracy and Multimedia Expansion (1983–2002) 37
Defensive Concentration (2002–2008) 41
War against CFK (2008–2015) 43
Mega-merger and Tailor-made Rules (2015–2020) 46
   Zoon Politikon 49
Notes 51
References 52

3 Economic Profile — 54

Corporate Structure 54
    Capital Structure. Shareholders, Board of Directors and Management 56
Lines of Business and Market Share 62
Stages of the Integration Process 67
    Monomedia Expansion (1945–1988) 67
    Multimedia Expansion (1989–2006) 71
    Clarín's Journey to Convergence (2007–2015) 77
    Grupo Clarín in 2016–2020: "The First Argentine Holding of Converged Communications" 84
New Business Lines and Digital Restructuring 88
Seventy-Five Years of Grupo Clarín 90
Notes 91
References 93
Interview 95

4 Cultural Profile of *Clarín* — 96

Introduction 96
1945–1969: The Noble Era 97
1969–1982: Developmentalism, a National View of Culture 101
1982–2001: The Consolidation of the Cross-Media Conglomerate 105
2001–2009: Recovery and National Culture 113
2009–2020: Confrontation and Metamorphosis 118
Culture for All 122
Notes 123
References 124
Interviews 125

Conclusion — 126

Governments Have Passed. Clarín Has Stayed. What Might Its Future Look Like? 126
References 134

Index — 135

Figures

1	Grupo Clarín structure	57
2	Grupo Clarín shareholders	58
3	CVH shareholders	58
4	Telecom Argentina shareholders	59
5	Clarín & Telecom management structure	61
6	Market share – fixed broadband	63
7	Market share – pay TV	64
8	Market share – mobile lines	64
9	Aggregate audiences for press and broadcasting	65
10	Market share – programming channels	66
11	Market share – aggregate audiences AM-FM radio stations	66
12	Clarín's first phase of expansion (1945–1988)	70
13	Clarín's second phase of expansion (1989–2006)	76
14	Participation by business line (2007–2017)	79
15	Evolution of Clarín share (2008–2020)	81
16	Clarín Group price per share (2007–2016)	82
17	Clarín's fourth phase of expansion (2016–2020)	85
18	Share per business line (2018–2019)	86

Tables

1	Newspaper sales	70
2	Payment of dividends	83
3	Revenues per business line (2007–2019)	87

Introduction

This book examines Grupo Clarín, Argentina's most significant cross-media conglomerate, through a comprehensive journey across its historical, political, economic, technological and cultural dimensions.

Grupo Clarín is the dominant group in the media and telecommunications landscape in Argentina. It stands out for being the only actor in the local market with a footprint that spans the broadcast TV, pay TV, radio, newspaper, magazine, paper manufacturing, broadband connectivity and fixed and mobile telecom market segments, with a leading position across them all. Notably, it is in the lead not only in terms of the scope of its product and service delivery but also in terms of revenues, territorial coverage and the impact on audiences and users.

Over a period of 75 years, from the creation of the newspaper *Clarín* in 1945 by Roberto Noble to the present day, the company turned into a conglomerate and a leading player in the news, entertainment and communications production system of Argentina, notable for its capacity to influence media policymaking and regulation, the market structure, and cultural practices and consumption. Hence, its importance as an object of study within the Global Media Giants (GMG) series, taking a political economy approach and enabling a multidimensional analysis.

This book draws on a combination of data gathering techniques and the review of previous research on Grupo Clarín, communication policies in Argentina and the Latin American region and documents that mapped the country's political cycles and economy. Documentary sources also include the company's annual performance reports, other corporate reports and statistics issued by public agencies. A third set of sources includes in-depth interviews with the Group's executives, with journalists and other professionals who worked at the various Grupo Clarín entities in different stages throughout its existence, and with researchers who have studied the evolution of this business conglomerate.

The growth of the business group that today is Grupo Clarín started in the 1970s, when *Clarín* newspaper began its process of vertical expansion. Its starting point was the creation of the news agency *Diarios y Noticias* (DyN) – shut down in 2017 – and the establishment of a partnership with the Argentine state – in the midst of the military dictatorship – and with two other journalistic companies to run the only paper mill for the country's newspapers, called Papel Prensa. In the 1980s, the Group diversified, first entering into the radio industry and then into the free-to-air TV space. During the 1990s, it deployed an aggressive expansion strategy in the pay TV and internet service provision segments of the market, while partnering with content production companies and even making a fleeting foray into the mobile phone market. It was the decade of Grupo Clarín's formal debut as the entity it had come to be – a multimedia group. In the first decade of the 21st century, it solidified its position in the delivery of bundled cable and internet services, placing high bets on the digitization of its signals. In 2016, Grupo Clarín entered the mobile communications market, first with the acquisition of Nextel and then with the mega-merger of Cablevisión (its cable TV operator) and Telecom Argentina, and thus took the lead in both mobile communications and the broadband connectivity market.

This consolidation process galvanized as different stages unfolded in Argentine history, and found support in the public policies of administrations that differed in their political colors but favored Grupo Clarín's growth.

The main strength of Grupo Clarín was its prowess to cope with the ups and downs of national politics and to keep up the threat – at times latent, at times explicit – of waging conflicts against whatever or whoever stood in the way of its plans. Such prowess is also evident in the Group's cultural profile, defined as multi-target and multi-class, although its rationale of economic accumulation and the ensuing search for political legitimacy took precedence over its cultural value proposition.

In general, and with nuances depending on the administration in office, it may be claimed that until 2008, the various governments were responsive to the Group's demands. This relationship, however, reached a turning point during the two Cristina Fernández de Kirchner (2007–2015) administrations. One of the expressions of this conflict was the process of debate and enactment of the Audiovisual Communication Services Law in 2009. Later on, with the arrival of Mauricio Macri to the presidency in December 2015, Grupo Clarín found significant support, with regulations enabling it to take a new and major leap in its expansion process in the telecommunications sphere and reach extraordinary dimensions, even outdoing other significant groups at the regional level. Its dominant position in the telecom networks space gave it economic power to become a key player in the landscape of converged communications.

Several studies have focused on examining the development of Grupo Clarín, as well as the figure of its legendary CEO and main shareholder, Hector Magnetto, who has been at the helm of the Group setting its course of expansion for four decades. Among the main critical studies on the economic and political dimensions of Grupo Clarín, Sivak (2013 and 2015), Mochkofsky (2011) and Ramos (1993) have all explored its establishment as a multimedia group. Also noteworthy are the PhD theses of Borrelli (2011) and Levín (2009), both focusing on the latest dictatorship, the former analyzing *Clarín* newspaper's position on economic policy during that period and the latter dealing with its graphic humor.

Moreover, there are books that portray the Group's official voice and focus on the figure of Magnetto (López, 2008 and Magnetto, 2017), as well as an unauthorized biography of Ernestina Herrera de Noble, the widow of *Clarín* newspaper's founder (Llonto, 2003).

Likewise, a number of research papers on communication policies and the structure of cultural industries in Argentina and Latin America have studied the consolidation process of Grupo Clarín (Albornoz, 2000; Getino, 2008; Becerra and Mastrini, 2009, 2017; Mastrini, 2009; Mastrini and Becerra, 2006, 2017; among others).

Acknowledging these sources, this book makes a distinctive contribution by addressing Grupo Clarín from the perspective of the political economy of media, linking its political, economic and cultural dimensions, while also considering the technological transformations it went through. The political economy of media analyzes changes in the value chain of cultural industries, their impact on business models and the transformations in policies and regulations; hence, it provides tools to understand the relationship of the media system with society and power (Zallo, 2011).

As a large conglomerate, Grupo Clarín has leverage capacity on both the economy and the symbolic configurations of society, and, for that reason, it is relevant as a case study for its considerable power to influence the policymaking process for the communications sector nationwide.

A distinctive feature of Grupo Clarín compared to other regional giants such as Televisa in Mexico is that its owners do not have direct political affiliations or parliamentary involvement to influence policymaking in the sector. In that respect, the Group's dynamic resembles more that of Grupo Globo in Brazil, whose owners have tried to stay close to almost all governments.

Another differentiator of Clarín, in this case vis-à-vis both Televisa and Globo, is the speed and aggressiveness with which it has managed to overcome regulatory, economic and market definition obstacles to become the dominant group in print media, broadcasting (radio and TV), pay TV and telecommunications.

A third distinctive trait that sets it apart from other large regional groups is its shareholding composition. Even though Grupo Clarín has maintained the characteristics of a family-run business group typical of Latin American conglomerates, instead of following the patriarchal line of succession after the death of Mr. Noble, the newspaper's founder, it was his widow, Ernestina Herrera, that took the helm, followed by her children, Marcela and Felipe. Also noteworthy is the fact that a person who is unrelated to the family lineage, Mr. Magnetto, leads the company's management, both at the executive and at the shareholding level.

Different authors have emphasized that technological changes in the media should be considered in the context of the web of social and cultural relations associated with a certain configuration of power (Williams, 1992; Castells, 2009; Zallo, 2011). Thus, in the face of political changes, technology disruptions and the challenges posed by global players for traditional media business models, the Grupo Clarín case study is also relevant to understand the strategies deployed in a scenario of digital convergence and how such corporate practices affect society.

The book comprises four chapters. Following this introduction, the first chapter includes a historical tour through key aspects of Argentine political and economic evolution, as well as the dynamics of state intervention on the media, as a way to approach the history of Grupo Clarín.

The second chapter deals with the political dimension, showing as a persistent thread the Group's ability to articulate actions with the different governments (both civil and military), while relying on economic aspects to enable its business to thrive. It also explains how in the last 20 years the Group adopted more comfortable and aggressive positions to confront government obstacles that conditioned the expansive dynamics of the conglomerate. This line of action had consequences in terms of the subordination of journalistic production and cultural content to an expansive project of Grupo Clarín as a corporation.

The third chapter delves into the Group's economic profile, examining its business structure, lines of business and the journey through its four moments of expansion that illustrate its strategy relying on indebtedness and reinvestment within the communications sector: 1945–1988, the monomedia stage of expansion; 1989–2006, the multimedia stage; 2007–2015, the bet on infrastructure and digitization; and 2016–2020, full convergence. The latest stage, marked by the Cablevisión-Telecom merger, fully accounts for the central role played by the networks in the Group's growth strategy.

The fourth chapter dives into the Group's cultural project, comprising five profiles. Between 1945 and 1969, under Noble's leadership, the tenets of the newspaper pointed to an agile and popular culture that brought along a steady increase in sales. Between 1969 and 1982, Rogelio Frigerio's idea of culture prevailed, in conjunction with the broader geopolitical vision of this leader. Between 1982 and 2001, a notion of culture subject to business criteria and the consolidation of a culturally multi-target group predominated. Between 2001 and 2009, Grupo Clarín focused on the reconstruction of its damaged financials and a cultural profile that was more closely linked to the national agenda. Finally, in recent years and due to the strong confrontation with the two Cristina Fernández de Kirchner administrations, the target audience shifted, with cultural approaches shaped by a more marked ideological bias. The common denominator throughout these stages was the focus on a massive audience.

Following the four chapters, a Conclusions section at the end of the book includes some final thoughts on the development of Grupo Clarín over its 75-year history, and addresses potential questions about its future.

References

Albornoz, Luis (Coord.) (2000). *Al fin solos. La nueva televisión del Mercosur*. Buenos Aires, Argentina: Editorial Ciccus- La Crujía.

Becerra, Martín and Guillermo Mastrini (2009). *Los dueños de la palabra: acceso, estructura y concentración de los medios en la América latina del siglo XXI*. Buenos Aires: Prometeo Libros.

Becerra, Martín and Guillermo Mastrini (2017). *La concentración infocomunicacional en América Latina (2000–2015). Nuevos medios y tecnologías, menos actores*. Bernal: UNQ -OBSERVACOM.

Borrelli, Marcelo (2011). *El diario Clarín frente a la política económica de Martínez de Hoz (1976–1981)*, mimeo, doctoral thesis presented in the PhD of the Social Science Department of the UBA.

Castells, Manuel (2009). "La comunicación en la era digital", in *Comunicación y Poder* (pp. 87–189). Madrid: Alianza Editorial.
Getino, Octavio (2008). *El capital de la cultura. Las industrias culturales en la Argentina*. Buenos Aires: Editorial Ciccus.
Levín, Florencia (2009). *La realidad al cuadrado: Representaciones sobre lo político en el humor gráfico del diario Clarín (1973–1983)*. Thesis to opt for the degree of PhD in History. Philosophy Department, Universidad de Buenos Aires. http://repositorio.filo.uba.ar/handle/filodigital/1408
Llonto, Pablo (2003). *La noble Ernestina*. Buenos Aires: Punto de encuentro.
López, José (2008). *El hombre de Clarín. Vida pública y privada de Héctor Magnetto*. Buenos Aires: Sudamericana.
Magnetto, Héctor (2017). *Así lo viví. El poder, los medios y la política en Argentina*. Buenos Aires: Planeta.
Mastrini, Guillermo (ed.) (2009). *Mucho ruido, pocas leyes: economía y políticas de comunicación en la Argentina*. Buenos Aires: La Crujía.
Mastrini, Guillermo and Martín Becerra (2006). *Periodistas y Magnates. Estructura y concentración de las industrias culturales en América Latina*. Buenos Aires: Prometeo Libros.
Mastrini, Guillermo and Martín Becerra (eds.) (2017). *Medios en guerra: balance, crítica y desguace de las políticas de comunicación 2003–2016*. Buenos Aires: Biblos.
Mochkofsky, Graciela (2011). *Pecado original. Clarín, los Kirchner y la lucha por el poder*. Buenos Aires: Planeta.
Ramos, Julio (1993). *Los cerrojos de la prensa*. Buenos Aires: Editorial Amfin.
Sivak, Martín (2013). *Clarín. Una historia*. Buenos Aires: Planeta.
Sivak, Martín (2015). *Clarín. La era Magnetto*. Buenos Aires: Planeta.
Williams, Raymond (ed.) (1992). "Tecnologías de la información e instituciones sociales", in *Historia de la comunicación* (pp. 182–210). Barcelona: editorial Bosch.
Zallo, Ramón (2011). "Retos actuales de la economía crítica de la comunicación y la cultura", in Albornoz, L. (comp.). *Poder, Medios, Cultura. Una mirada crítica desde la economía política de la comunicación* (pp. 17–60). Buenos Aires: Paidós.

1 Understanding *Clarín*
An Overview of Argentine History

Introduction

Grupo Clarín was founded in 1945 in Argentina, a southern peripheral country. One of the main characteristics that have always been present throughout the country's history is the highly volatile political and economic scene, which has included on and off periods of military dictatorships and democratic governments up until 1983. To put this in perspective in the political sphere, Argentina has recently experienced its first full uninterrupted cycle of democratically elected governments; however, in the economic sphere, instability has persisted.

In this chapter, we will elaborate on key elements of the various Argentine political and economic processes in order to better understand the context in which a small newspaper became one of the biggest cross-media conglomerates in the region. The Group's history can be divided into two periods. *Clarín*'s build-up and expansion process from 1945 to 1985 was marked by the consolidation of its original market, print media. From 1985 until today, the Group undertook rapid media expansion, allowing it to develop telecommunications and connectivity convergence since 2007. What sets Grupo Clarín apart from the other main media groups in Latin America (such as Televisa and Globo) is its late expansion. These other media outlets managed to expand their multimedia operations between 1960 and 1970, long before the Argentine newspaper.

The next chapter will discuss *Clarín*'s ability to politically connect with both civil and military governments. In its early years, the newspaper established strong ties with a political party (the Integration and Development Movement or MID), which briefly attained the presidency between 1958 and 1962. However, since 1980, *Clarín* drifted apart from the MID, and its editorial policy became less doctrinal and more opportunistic. During the 1990s, the Carlos Menem administration's neoliberal approach played a key role in adapting legislation to the needs of emerging media groups. Since then, Grupo Clarín has managed to always remain at the forefront regarding the development of new markets: First, it entered the world of cable TV, then it ventured into the internet industry, and finally, it set foot in cross-media services by introducing landline and mobile communications. Excluding the 2009–2015 period, Grupo Clarín's ability to influence key regulations was paramount for the newspaper's expansion, and allowed for implicit – rather than explicit – agreements with different governments.

Even though Argentina's economic instability has not posed a major obstacle for the Group's development, it can be regarded as one of the elements that restrained its international expansion, alongside the country's relatively small market (45 million citizens in 2020) and the lack of credit in national currency. All of these aspects had an impact on the Group, which obtained most of its income from the domestic market. As a response, its CEO, Héctor Magnetto, took on a strategic approach: In the new media world, you either grow or disappear.

An overview of the political and economic context of Argentina – focusing especially on state intervention in the media – allows for a better understanding of *Clarín's* political, economic and cultural profile.

1945–1955. Peronism, the Media and *Clarín*

The first coup d'état in the history of Argentina took place in 1930. Between then and 1943, the country saw a succession of conservative governments that failed to solve the conflict between the agro-export and industrial sectors within the hegemonic bloc. Furthermore, neither of those governments succeeded in reducing the high tensions arising from Argentina's political position regarding World War II. In 1943, another military coup took place instigated by a nationalistic group that sided with the Axis powers, which also presented important inconsistencies in terms of both economic policies and international relations. A young Colonel, Juan Domingo Perón, first Secretary of Labor and later on Vice President, participated in the coup of 1943, setting the stage for the emergence of a new party of the masses. His policies gave the state more control over the media, especially radio broadcasting, which at the time was the main mass media.

After a popular outbreak, the then Military President Edelmiro Farrell held an election that was won comfortably by Perón. His administrations (1946–1952 and 1952–1955)[1] brought about major economic and political change. Strongly supported by the working class – which

Understanding Clarín 9

reached unprecedented levels of unionization all over Latin America – Peronism's goal was to increase import substitution by boosting the levels of industrialization. To fund this plan, there was a significant redistribution of resources, international meat and grains trade was nationalized, and import duties were levied. Peronism used these revenues to fund industrial development. Moreover, Perón's administration initiated a redistribution of income in favor of the working classes – a move that was very popular among wage workers, who felt better represented by the state, while the more traditional power sectors, including landowners, strongly opposed the move. Certainly, what is regarded as "First Peronism" constituted one of the most controversial Argentine periods that still remain remarkably polarizing. Eduardo Basualdo, an economist that has close ties with Peronism, described the period in the following way:

> The 1944–1955 period witnessed a divide in terms of economic, social and political development. The first Peronist administrations set in motion an unprecedented experience by combining economic growth with a major increase in the workers' share of income. Studies about these periods point to the existence of a rapid economic expansion based on the exceptional situation involving the balance of payments – which originated in the midst of the global conflict – and on a significant increase in gross fixed investment. However, in the context of the rapid industrial growth that put an end to the agro-export model, the first Peronist administrations were special in that they incorporated the working class in social, political and economic terms.
> (Basualdo, 2010: 34)

On a more orthodox note, Gerchunoff and Llach did not mince words to criticize the Peronist model:

> The diversified industrial policies chosen by Peronism were particularly troubling in a country with a relatively small population such as Argentina. Many industries that emerged as a result of the protectionist policies of the 1940s and 1950s failed to reach the right scale that would allow them to work efficiently – a problem that could have been mitigated by a more selective industrialization process. The increased demand for workers was bound to cause an increase in wages because there was a lack of sufficient 'reserve forces' in the agricultural sector. From the industrialists' standpoint, this increase in wages – coupled with other labor costs

stemming from the Peronist welfare state – would soon become a concern.

(Gerchunoff and Llach, 1998: 218)

While Peronism was marked by an increase in state involvement on the economic front, the administration's interventionist features that began under the previous government regarding media policies deepened. Furthermore, through a series of tax credits and political pressures, the state came to indirectly control the three big broadcast networks and most of the country's newspapers. Their management of a scarce resource, newsprint paper,[2] was key when it came to influencing the printed press. In the next chapter, we will discuss how newcomer *Clarín* managed to get close enough to Peronism to obtain the prized material.

In 1951, Peronism launched the first TV station controlled by the state. Nevertheless, many years would pass before TV replaced radio as the media of choice in people's everyday life.

In 1950, the industrialization process started to show signs of exhaustion due to the lack of investment and, even though Perón was supported by a large part of the population, he was overthrown by a military coup in 1955.

Cycle of Political Unrest

The majority of coup supporters assumed they were helping bring the political party created by Perón to an end. However, their expectations were frustrated by the events that unfolded in contemporary Argentine history. On the one hand, Peronism had permanently modified the country's political and social scene. Its influence over popular sectors – which were now incorporated into the political sphere – extended over the following decades. On the other hand, inconsistencies soon began to emerge within the winning party. Even though the opposition unified, major disagreements arose within the coalition: National Catholics, liberals, radicals and socialists – everyone had their own thoughts on both Peronism and the country. A great struggle ensued between conservative nationalism and anti-Peronist liberal sectors. Furthermore, radicalism and socialism played their bets on a speedy return of governments legitimized by the popular vote – even if it meant the banning of the Peronist party.

Additionally, Peronism had left a permanent mark on the country's economy. The aggressive industrialist path encouraged by Perón and Argentina's economic transformation – along with an industrial production that exceeded agricultural production – was to survive despite its nuances for two more decades. Although a significant number of members of the dictatorship that took place between 1955 and 1958 had strong ties with the traditional agro-export oligarchy – even encouraging a return to the economic model of 19th-century Argentina – it no longer had the ability to lead the masses: First, due to the resistance offered by workers through their union representatives, and second, because the world economy had gone through major transformations and the value of raw materials had fallen. The economic plan presented by Raúl Prebisch – who was by then serving as executive director of the Economic Commission for Latin America and the Caribbean (ECLAC) – was meant to propel a second level of industrialization through economic policies that, in time, would become recurring: Privatizations and wage control. A serious challenge for the Argentine economy had to do with the lack of an industrial bourgeoisie capable of providing the necessary capital to boost the development process. Instead, the small bourgeoisie that emerged during the Peronist era appeared to be incapable of leading such movement. By then, the administration began to consider the alternative of increasing foreign investment. Meanwhile, both political tensions and economic hardships also had an impact on economic policies regarding cultural industries.

When Arturo Frondizi was elected president (1958–1962), a process took place that included both short-term governments elected by the people and military governments that barged in through coups until they were once again compelled to call for elections. Although it would be very difficult to summarize the variety of political forces of the time, the so-called "military party" was made up of the agro-export sector, nationalist Catholicism and political conservatism. At the other end were the timid industrial bourgeoisie and the unions that were directly linked to banned Peronism. While the former group had more economic power, the latter had more social and political power. This situation – which gave the workforce an increased share in the distribution of domestic income almost at par with capital – was described by Juan Carlos Portantiero (1989) as a "hegemonic draw."

Frondizi went for the continuation of the industrialization process that began with Perón. For its second phase, he opened up the economy to foreign investment. Nevertheless, his political project failed to solidify in the midst of pressures by the Peronist branch that had supported it and the "military party." In 1962, Frondizi was overthrown by another coup.

Beyond Frondizi's administration, the 1960s saw significant political and social changes. During this period, a certain cultural, ideologic, theoretic and political climate was conceived – in its broadest sense – which is a phenomenon that rarely occurs throughout history. On an ideological – and oftentimes political – level, there was a unique degree of radicalization that did not repeat itself in the following decades and which was linked, especially, to the Peronist movement. After Perón's second mandate was overthrown in 1955, the heterodox and multi-class political movement he once led was banned until 1973. Over those 18 years, a social phenomenon ensued, known as the *peronization* of middle-class sectors, which involved the massive integration of youth from the middle class to the ranks of the movement called Peronist Youth (*Juventud Peronista*, JP). Moreover, various Marxist groups were established, which in some cases would resort to armed conflicts.

After the coup against Frondizi, Arturo Illia's Radical Civic Union (*Unión Cívica Radical, UCR*) won the 1963 elections, while Peronism was still banned. In 1966, a new coup d'état seized power, which self-identified as the "Argentine Revolution." This military dictatorship did not present itself as a provisional government and its management style was later described by Guillermo O'Donnell as a "bureaucratic-authoritarian state" (O'Donnell, 1982). During the dictatorship, the relationship between the urban middle-class youth and national liberation movements deepened as they kept joining these political groups. The high levels of political and social tension during the Argentine Revolution – as well as the clash between several military sectors – brought forth two internal coups that resulted in a succession of three different Military Presidents: Juan Carlos Onganía (1966–1970), Roberto Levingston (1970–1971) and Alejandro Lanusse (1971–1973). Finally, amid growing social unrest, the dictatorship put together an electoral exit in 1973 without imposing a ban on Peronism for the first time in 18 years.

On March 11, 1973, on behalf of Perón, Héctor Cámpora won at the polls as leader of the FREJULI (Justicialist Liberation Front) with 49.5 percent of the votes. However, shortly thereafter, Cámpora resigned, enabling Perón to run for president in a new electoral process with his wife, María Estela Martínez de Perón, as Vice President. Within months, Perón took office after obtaining 62 percent of the votes – the highest number of votes ever secured by a presidential candidate in Argentine history.

As Peronism returned in the midst of tensions between the agro-export model and the import substitution model, the political balance tipped in favor of the latter. Furthermore, amid the capital-labor struggle, the alliance between the national bourgeoisie and workforce sectors regained strength, as both had suffered during the second half of the 1960s from an industrialization process that relied on foreign capital (Basualdo, 2010: 95).

Peronism attempted to get back to the roots of Perón's first administration. Therefore, it promoted a national consensus between unions and national business owners that involved recovering salaries while committing to a raise in productivity in order to avoid an inflationary surge.

Upon returning to office, Peronism did not go back to placing the state at the center of the industrial expansion plan, but rather turned it into a guarantee for the different economic interest groups. However, especially after Perón's death in 1974, the state failed to maintain the multi-class alliance it intended to promote. The economic crisis, which deepened in 1975, together with the climate of political violence that riddled the country, paved the way for yet another military coup that took place in 1976.

This extended period of political unrest was reflected on media policies. The government that overthrew Perón in 1955 arranged for the media to be returned to their previous owners, which in the case of *La Prensa* newspaper was done immediately. As regards radio broadcasters, the process was slow and inconclusive. By the end of the 1950s, private television was established under one main condition: Broadcast owners had to certify they did not maintain ties with Peronism. The invitation to tender that was issued in 1958 was won by three local groups that, in 1960, forged an alliance with the three major television networks of the United States, which provided the necessary capital to deploy private TV. However, although Argentine successful bidders were the owners of the networks, foreign investors assumed control over the economy and the contents. Due to the direct ownership of production companies and the indirect ownership of the networks, ABC, NBC and CBS achieved vertical integration and distribution of contents – which was forbidden in the United States. *Clarín,* which was in the process of establishing itself as a print media, was yet to enter the radio and TV industries.

The 1960s witnessed prosperous times for print media and the publishing industry, and was also a time of exploration and recognition regarding the film industry. Within this framework, the companies behind the new networks became the spearhead of media modernization (Varela, 2005: 117).

Starting in 1965, the three large US networks began withdrawing from private stations. To summarize the events between 1955 and 1973, it can be said that the 1960s marked the consolidation of Argentine television. Even though by the time private TV was introduced the state-run *Canal 7* had been airing for ten years, it was definitively established as a mass media outlet with the emergence of commercial broadcasters, which coincided with the consumption boom of household appliances by the middle and working classes. While private TV was still in development, consumption of print media increased in the middle and lower sectors. In that light, *Clarín* was able to solidify its revenue stream and get back on its financial feet.

The return of Peronism to power (1973–1976) was as intense and controversial regarding audiovisual policies as it was in political and economic terms. In October 1973, Acting President Raúl Lastiri[3] signed a decree (1761/1773) declaring TV licenses owned by the main Argentine stations obsolete (channels 9, 11 and 13 in Buenos Aires, 8 in Mar del Plata and 7 in Mendoza). After a lengthy process, in 1975 the main TV broadcasters came under state control. The nationalization of Argentine TV was paramount for Grupo Clarín history, because, following the return to democracy in 1983, the company would push toward privatization and present itself as one of the major contenders for the acquisition of some of the stations.

The Dictatorship and the Media: Control and Privatization

The dictatorship that followed the 1976 coup d'état carried out a carefully designed economic, political and social transformation project. The self-proclaimed "National Reorganization Process" had a clear objective: Recreate the politically conservative and economically liberal policies of the 19th-century agro-export oligarchy of Argentina. Over that period, the military dictatorship (1976–1983) exercised state terrorism, destroyed the existing "hegemonic draw," and put an end to the dichotomy between the agricultural and industrial sectors. Instead, it promoted a model based on financial profitability that translated into an intense deindustrialization process. This political, economic and cultural project adopted a neoliberal approach, and pursued cultural policies controlled by the military that involved civilian participants for its layout, management, application and development.

As Gerchunoff and Llach point out, Minister of Economy José Martínez de Hoz developed an economic plan that proposed the vindication of the private sector, the suppression of the fiscal deficit and the repeal of export duties, mainly for agricultural exports. In their own words: "The intellectual consensus that emerged during the 1960s, coupled with such notions as Keynesianism, Welfare State and full employment, quickly derived into a twilight phase" (Gerchunoff and Llach, 1998: 353). Basically, the economic policies implemented by the dictatorship led to a fall in real wages and to a mild de-escalation of the inflationary process (which was never lower than 1 percent per month). However, its major economic impact reflected on the reform of the financial sector, which involved freeing the interest rate and the denationalization of deposits – i.e., less intervention of the Central Bank in the money market. This rampant liberalization process led to an increase in financial speculation that resulted in many banks going bankrupt or being bailed out by the state.

Basualdo characterized the period on the basis of the enforcement of a new accumulation model:

> Through state terrorism exercised by the military dictatorship, dominant sectors enforced a new pattern of capital accumulation that had economic policies and a whole new attitude on the part of the state at its core. This new approach resulted in the validation of the financial valuation of part of the surplus appropriated by the oligopolistic capital by acquiring various financial assets (such as securities, bonds and deposits) in both the internal and external markets. At the time, interest rates exceeded the profitability of economic activities and the rapid growth of the country's foreign debt made it possible to send local capital abroad.
> (Basualdo, 2010: 117)

This dramatic economic restructuring, which involved a significant redistribution of income in favor of capital, would have never been possible without a terror regime sheltering such policies. By the end of the dictatorship, the country was heavily indebted and its industrial apparatus was almost completely destroyed.

Meanwhile, the military relied on other control tactics apart from raw strength. During the dictatorship, strong media policies were implemented, which allowed for the use of Argentina's broadcasting system to mount a major propaganda campaign. Their influence over the media was such that, during the Military Junta's 19th statement – on the night of March 24, 1976 – the government already talked about censorship and subsequent punishment. Thus, the mass media played a key role, as the administration exercised control over the main TV channels (which were vested in the state since before the coup) and radio broadcasters.

Argentina's major newspapers – including *Clarín* – supported the coup and embraced the censorship imposed on the media. Eventually, private media started practicing self-censorship. The country's big media outlets refrained from any discussion about important topics such as military violence, torture and the disappearance of thousands of people; whenever those subjects surfaced, it was to convey the administration's position on the matter. Despite censorship and declining public consumption, these were good years for *Clarín*, which managed to consolidate as Argentina's best-selling newspaper.

The alliance between the main media outlets and the dictatorship went beyond content. What transpired between the country's newsprint manufacturer, Papel Prensa, and the dictatorship clearly exemplifies the partnership arranged by the military government and Argentina's main newspapers. In the midst of the dictatorship, Papel Prensa went back into production after years of postponements, and its share package was distributed among four partners: the state, and *Clarín, La Nación* and *La Razón* newspapers. The share transfer took place at the price of 8 million dollars and the government itself funded its brand-new associates by granting them loans through the National Development Bank. Additionally, the companies received a large subsidy on their energy consumption, while import duties on paper were raised to 48 percent. Thus, an oligopoly was secured that has managed – and still manages – the price of newsprint paper at will.

The Return to Democracy: Alfonsín, Menem and De la Rúa

Raúl Alfonsín's Radical Civic Union (UCR)[4] won the elections in October 1983, in an unpredictable victory over the Peronist party, which had dominated presidential races since its beginnings in 1946. Although the return to democracy and Alfonsín's own charisma elicited high expectations, the challenges faced by the new administration were considerable. The country's economy suffered from regressive policies that persisted due to Argentina's huge foreign debt – which turned out to be one of the major constraints on Argentine economic policies for decades.

The economic policy pursued by the radical government was divided into two well-defined stages. During the first year and a half, the country attempted to renegotiate its foreign debt along with other countries of the region and to recover the purchasing power of wages. Mainly, the administration pushed toward recreating the re-industrialization process, thus making a 180-degree turn compared to the policies of the dictatorship. Basualdo condemns the actions taken by the UCR because they did not consider the profound changes made by the previous administration:

> Foreign creditors and concentrated national capital – which, from then on, comprised foreign conglomerates and local economic

groups – went on to dominate the economic process by overexploiting workers and exercising control over the state to pursue their particular interests. The accumulation process was based on financial value and, therefore, was no longer conditioned by the consumption of popular sectors and national frontiers, thus prompting the dissolution of the national industrial capital that had established various alliances with the working class in order to boost industrial development.

(Basualdo, 2001: 39)

During the second stage, the government backed down on its attempts to protect salaries and channeled its efforts toward reducing inflation and paying for the country's foreign debt. In 1985, Juan Sourrouille replaced Bernardo Grinspun as Minister of Economy and emphasized the need to respond to international requests, renegotiate payments in arrears and refinance the debt in the long term. After some initial success, the plan dried up in just a couple of years and, in 1988, a hyperinflationary process began that would prematurely put an end to Alfonsín's administration.

Comprehending the nature of Argentina's inflationary crisis during those years is of vital importance, not just because it was a very atypical process, but also because it would determine society's behavior in the years to come. Furthermore, the crisis entailed a serious disruption to the usual cyclical crises that arose during the development of the substitution model: It aimed at removing structural restrictions that hampered the development and consolidation of the accumulation pattern based on the notion of financial value that had been installed by the dictatorship.

While, politically, the radical government drifted through a sea of contradictions between its intentions and the restrictions dictated by unfavorable circumstances, media policies were affected by limitations that were typical of their administration. Even though the government ceased the implementation of authoritarian policies inherited by the dictatorship, it was not capable of establishing a new set of media policies. In the meantime, the Argentine broadcasting system appeared to be stuck in time and had substantively remained the same since 1960. Later on, radical changes would come along during Carlos Menem's administration through media policies and the transformation of the economic sector.

During Alfonsín's administration, the constant tensions between Grupo Clarín and the government were palpable. While the Group's objective was to venture into the audiovisual sector through acquisitions and privatizations, Radicalism's idleness on the matter slowed down the concentration of media ownership pursued by Grupo Clarín's executives.

Meanwhile, newspaper sales increased and *Clarín* presented itself as the great Argentine newspaper. Furthermore, the economic establishment of the press allowed Grupo Clarín to accumulate the necessary capital to set foot into the audiovisual sector.

Ultimately, cable TV managed to grow as it expanded from the provinces into the City of Buenos Aires. Through investments made by hundreds of medium-size companies, a cable TV network was established that, in 1990, would be absorbed by large conglomerates – including Grupo Clarín.

The following administrations used the hyperinflationary crisis to introduce structural changes laying the foundations for the accumulation pattern that had developed under the dictatorship: Financial value, privatizations and "free market."

In the 1989 elections, Peronism came back to power, this time under the leadership of Carlos Menem. Although during his political campaign he promised to follow in the footsteps of the party's traditional policies in favor of industrialization, his administration's economic agenda was completely opposite.

Menem took the lessons learned from Argentina's latest crisis and quickly channeled his efforts toward handling it, as he favored the interests of large economic groups from the very beginning. Once he took office, Menem implemented the directives that multinational financial institutions (IMF, the World Bank) had been requiring for a long time: Developing a rapid program of privatization of public companies, implementing a substantial tax reform and encouraging a financial reform that would completely free the flow of capital.

In this context, the privatization of public companies was vital, because the new private enterprises constituted common ground between national and foreign capital.

Nevertheless, inflation could not be brought to a standstill and the economic crisis still lurked around. In 1991, the country's economic policies took a turn when Domingo Cavallo became Minister of Economy and pushed toward currency convertibility of the Argentine peso, which – after a significant devaluation – remained tied to the US dollar[5] for a decade. The measures taken by Cavallo, which implied giving up any possibility of having a monetary policy, were at least useful in considerably reducing inflation.

Furthermore, the whole picture included a program known as the Brady Plan – developed in 1992 – which entailed the restructuring of the country's foreign debt owed to multilateral lending agencies.

Additionally, the Plan enabled Argentina to be reinserted in the global financial system. The opening of international credit helped usher in the "golden years of neoliberal policies," as the domestic market's accessible credit allowed for consumption growth. This period of economic "bonanza" stimulated the growth of the Argentine economy between 1992 and 1994, and legitimized the country's economic model, as one of Argentina's most significant concentration and foreignization processes in history was consummated.

However, in the mid-1990s, the economic model started showing signs of exhaustion. The fiscal deficit and the balance of payments generated by the system (the former caused by the defunding of the welfare sector – which was privatized – and the latter, by the excessive boom of imports) were added to a serious social problem: Unemployment, which increased to a rate of nearly 20 percent.

In 1995, following a constitutional reform, Menem was reelected and served his second term in the midst of increasing economic difficulties. During the late 1990s, foreign capital concentrated in the financial and private services sectors while large national groups reduced their assets and limited their investments to agriculture. Amid the capital flight of the time, Argentine foreign debt increased exponentially, and the country could no longer afford a rise in productivity nor generate a trade surplus to match the US economy – with which it was tied to due to the established exchange rate parity. The country had to constantly resort to loans from multilateral lending agencies and to an increasing issuance of public debt. Such foreign indebtedness led to the severe 2001 economic crisis that stemmed from Argentina's inability to meet its payments, faced with the non-extension of outstanding credit. It is important to note that, at the time, the interests of national groups and of foreign capital clashed because of the breach caused by the transition between Menem's administrations.

Even though Menem managed to transfer the outburst of the crisis onto his successor, public opinion would regard him as the person responsible for one of the greatest economic depressions of Argentina. During the elections of October 1999, the Justicialist Party was defeated by an alliance led by the UCR, and Fernando de la Rúa became president.

De la Rúa's administration was unfit to solve the crisis it inherited. In 2001, his inability to pay for Argentina's foreign debt led to a default that, after a couple of months, brought about a steep devaluation of the Argentine peso. The social, political and economic crisis of the time was of such magnitude that it will not be forgotten for generations. In that context, De la Rúa had no choice but to step down. After brief interregnums, Senator Eduardo Duhalde took office, at the proposal of Peronism – which controlled the majority of Congress.

Menem's media policies were in tune with his administration's approach. The first substantial modifications were established by Act No. 23.696/89, known as the "State Reform Law," which enabled the privatization of public companies – including TV channels and radio broadcasters. Under the same Act, restrictions on print and audiovisual media cross-ownership were lifted, thus paving the way for the emergence of multimedia groups. The new legislation only limited the participation of foreign capital.

The privatization of TV channels was finalized in less than six months. None of the beneficiaries of the invitation to tender issued by Menem would have been able to bid under the old legislation enacted by Videla – which was partially amended by the State Reform Law. Grupo Clarín managed to obtain the license of Channel 13 and, additionally, it could launder *Radio Mitre*'s acquisition through straw buyers.

Following the privatization of TV channels, starting in 1990, the Executive Branch designed a comprehensive program to dispose of public assets. The privatization of the telecommunications sector was important because, just a few years later, it would become a key player in the cross-media industry.

In November, 1990, the company Entel was privatized and split into two different companies: One was taken over by Telefónica Argentina, which mainly partnered with Telefónica España, Citibank and local companies Techint and Perez Companc, and the other by Telecom, whose shareholders were the French and Italian state telephone companies, JP Morgan & Co. and Perez Companc. The alliances formed within the licensee groups that acquired public services companies reflect the combination of interests that determined the invitation to tender: International operators, bank creditors and large economic groups from Argentina (such as Techint and Perez Companc).

Almost a year into the Menem administration, Argentina's two most important TV channels and the country's telecommunications company had already been privatized. In both cases, the results reflect how important the modifications made to the previous regulatory framework were. Broadcasting and telecommunication services had separate legislation and, also, telephone companies were excluded from the audiovisual market.

Furthermore, an agreement was reached between the Argentine Football Association and Televisión Codificada SA that, starting in 1991, led to the commercial monopolization of soccer matches. The arrangement had an impact on the cable TV market, which took over soccer transmissions and adopted a dominant position in the market. The winning company that acquired the rights (which belonged to Carlos Ávila's Torneos y Competencias) along with ARTEAR (from Grupo Clarín) also took part in the distribution of cable TV services through the firm Multicanal.

In August 1992, Congress passed Act No. 24.124/192 that ratified the Agreement on Mutual Protection and Promotion of Investments with the United States, enabling the inflow of foreign capital into the media. Eventually, the agreement was supported by a constitutional reform that gave international treaties a higher rank than national laws, lifting the prohibition against the inflow of foreign capital that had been imposed by Videla's Broadcasting Decree-Law.

Since then, capital has flowed into the telecommunications and audiovisual sectors with an unprecedented dynamic of investments that included the increased participation of multinational financial capital and the subsequent concentration of media ownership. The growth of Foreign Direct Investment (FDI) recorded all over the Argentine economy reached the media sector, which saw the expenditure of 3 billion dollars on the acquisition of radio broadcasters, newspaper outlets and TV channels (Rossi, 2008).

The media policies of Menem's first administration were marked by the privatization process and by the legal modifications that fostered the development of commercial companies belonging to the audiovisual sector. By the end of his first term, the inflow of foreign capital was key to understanding one of the main characteristics of Menem's second term: The widening gap between the interests of national and international capitals.

Even though Menem's second administration was less prolific in terms of media policies, it would not forgo passing legislation in favor of the interests of affiliated groups. By passing Decree No. 1005/99, his administration favored certain focus groups by raising from 4 to 24 the maximum amount of licenses permitted per group. While at the beginning of his tenure Menem lifted the restrictions on the establishment of multimedia groups, by the end he legalized their expansion.

Kirchnerism

In 2003, after Duhalde's provisional government, Néstor Kirchner took office (2003–2007) and was followed by his wife, Cristina Fernández de Kirchner (CFK), who served two terms (2007–2011 and 2011–2015). Despite many internal disputes, their administrations extended over a 12-year period in which new economic and media policies were established.

During his provisional government, Duhalde had carried out a steep devaluation of the national currency and the price of the US dollar had soared. Consequently, certain sectors took up a new position within Argentina's economy, including the agricultural sector – which once again became an important grain exporter benefiting from the international value of commodities. Basically, the country's exploitation of soybean crops jump-started Argentina's ailing economy, which had left more than half the population living in poverty and the country in recession.

As early as his presidential inauguration, Kirchner's speech was critical of the neoliberalist period that preceded him and condemned the international bodies which had established economic parameters for the country.

When compared with the previous governments, Kirchner's administration set a different agenda that relied on the policies of the ever controversial center-left, or on the even more complex progressivism. His rhetoric was in favor of human rights, critical of the dictatorship and against the programs developed by the IMF and foreign banks. The administration's most important decisions included the replacement of Supreme Court members (introducing new judges with integrity and better records) and the development of a plan to overcome the economic default and tackle Argentina's debt with the IMF. Furthermore, Kirchner's administration vigorously pursued re-industrialist policies for certain sectors, and stimulated the recovery of the automobile and construction industries, both of which would bring about employment growth and an increase in domestic consumption. In turn, the financial sector and privatized public services companies – Menem's privileged partners – were demoted under the rule of the new administration and had to struggle to renegotiate their contracts and concessions.

Meanwhile, despite having obtained a swap and reduction from bondholders, the burden of Argentina's foreign debt was still heavy, as the country's main source of income continued to be the primary sector – chiefly the agroindustry, the oil industry and the expanding mining industry. Under this fragile scheme, the economy would get back on track and grow over the following years, stimulating a significant recovery of the GDP.

Kirchner's administration received a media system that was concentrated and heavily influenced by capital. His government also inherited an authoritative and centralized legal system that since 1983 –

and, especially, during the 1990s – strengthened those features. Although Kirchner's public rhetoric resorted to confronting with the framework established by the media, policies implied more continuities and agreements than modifications in favor of more inclusive or democratic media policies.

On June 18, 2003, less than a month after Néstor Kirchner's inauguration, Congress passed Law No. 25.750 for the "Preservation of Cultural Assets and Heritage" forbidding the acquisition of cultural companies by their external creditors – as was established by the Argentine Bankruptcy Law. In the authors' view, if the acquisition of other media companies is to be considered as the main cause of the media corporation's indebtedness – especially in the case of cable TV – this law could be interpreted as being protective of concentration of media ownership. This was particularly true for Grupo Clarín, which had funded its media expansion with debt in the previous decade.

In March 2005, Kirchner passed Necessity and Urgency Decree No. 527/05 – which was not included in the administration's public agenda – suspending the expiration date of broadcasting license terms for ten years and, once again, Grupo Clarín benefited from government actions. The same happened with the Law for the Preservation of Cultural Assets and Heritage, which reflected how the Argentine government yielded to the pressures of media corporations, without getting anything in return.

In August 2005, Act No. 26.053 was passed, allowing nonprofit organizations to provide cable TV services and apply for permits to broadcast on their local free-to-air TV channels and radio stations of limited range. Another progressive policy established at the time involved the strengthening of local media, including the creation of the educational channel *Encuentro*.

On his last day in office (12/07/2007), Kirchner authorized the merger between cable TV companies Cablevisión and Multicanal – both of which were placed under the control of Grupo Clarín. Cablevisión (which is also an internet service provider through the firm Fibertel) accounts for over 70 percent of the conglomerate's earnings. However, this symbiotic relationship between Kirchnerism and Grupo Clarín broke off the moment Cristina Fernández took office.

Roughly speaking, private media grew significantly during the Néstor Kirchner administration. The economic recovery over that period offered an excellent opportunity for main media corporations to get back on their feet after being on the verge of hitting rock bottom in 2002. Assessing the administration's main actions regarding media policies is key to assess the government's performance: While it was unwilling or unable to change the dictatorship's decree-law, it extended media license terms through legal (by granting renewals) and not so legal means (by passing DNU No. 527). Also, concentration of media ownership deepened over various sectors – as did the marginalization of certain players. The sector's legislation was once again passed through a decree, and state media – which was still recovering in terms of reach and quality – remained tied to the Executive Power's interests.

CFK's administrations are much more difficult to analyze than her husband's. The economic recovery and the growth of the GDP extended for a couple of years (even during the 2008 global crisis); yet the model started showing signs of exhaustion. The increase in domestic consumption encouraged by wage recovery fueled the rise of inflation, while, at the same time, the demand for imported goods for industrial neo-development restricted the availability of foreign exchange. In 2008, a fierce clash between Fernández de Kirchner and the agro-export sector broke out regarding the latter's tax rate contribution. The political consequence of the "crisis of the countryside" was an increasing disenchantment between Kirchnerism and the urban middle class. Throughout both of her terms (she was reelected in 2011, obtaining 54 percent of the votes), Cristina Fernández also questioned several other power structures (such as foreign banks, the media, the church and unions), as society divided between die-hard supporters and outraged opponents.

The confrontation between Kirchnerism and some of the country's main media outlets peaked in October 2009, when the Audiovisual Services Act No. 26.522 was passed. The change in media policies that took place in 2008 was very similar to other processes happening in other countries of the region, where civil groups active on the debate over the role of the media put forth reform proposals, which are later resumed by political powers when such initiatives are instrumental in a conflictive situation with certain players of concentrated media ownership.

Consequently, Act No. 26.522 went on to replace Decree-Law No. 22.285 of 1980, which had managed to survive for years after the dictatorship had come to an end. The new media legislation represented a major step forward, because it associated the concepts of freedom of speech and human rights. The Act – preceded by a heated social debate – encouraged the adoption of a federalist approach regarding the production of contents and decision-making processes. Additionally, it limited the concentration of media ownership and market dominance. Subsequently, for the first time, neither the enforcing authority nor the state media authority would be fully controlled by the government in power. Instead, checks and balances were established and political minorities were included – which was in line with progressive regulatory traditions. Grupo Clarín was especially affected by the limits imposed on the concentration of media ownership, which is why the passing of the law also meant the failure of the Group's powerful lobbying that, until the very last minute, thought it could block the legislation in Congress. Since then, Grupo Clarín became Fernández de Kirchner's sworn enemy and, for the first time in its history, the Group was persecuted by the state and fought back through its media outlets to weaken the government's position. However, in 2011, Cristina's reelection, coupled with Grupo Clarín's steady economic growth – despite being persecuted – reflects how ineffective both strategies were.

Recent Years

After 12 years in office, Kirchnerism was worn out and Peronism was divided (a branch of the party even ran for the presidency against them), paving the way for Mauricio Macri's victory in October 2015. For the first time in Argentine history, a right-wing alliance took office through free elections. The party's proposal combined the development of the agro-export sector with high value-added goods, including the software and renewable energies sectors. This approach implied abandoning the previous industrialist scheme based on extreme protectionism. Nevertheless, Macri's economic model lacked two things: Internal coherence and commitment, and heavy political weight (the party did not have a majority in Congress; thus, it was dependent on occasional alliances with moderate Peronists who followed suit when Macrism attempted to pass new legislation). After two years of steady growth caused by Argentina's return to the international credit market, the withdrawal of foreign funding of April 2018 plunged Macri's administration into an unrecoverable crisis that led to his losing the 2019 elections. Ultimately, Macrism did not achieve enough in terms of policies to narrow the social divide caused by the administration's decisions – especially in the case of marginalized masses of low-income citizens, which are frequent in Argentina and all of Latin America (Nun, 2010). The economic impact of Macri's administration was regressive for workers, whose share of income kept decreasing and which translated into rising unemployment and growing poverty. Thus, by the end of Macri's term, poverty amounted to over 30 percent of the population.

Even though Macrism sought to establish a convergent media policy, it did not go beyond isolated attempts on the matter. However, Macri's administration managed to restore (Becerra, 2016) a very favorable regulatory framework for the development of large media companies – especially Grupo Clarín.

In October 2019, Peronism defeated Macri and in December Alberto Fernández (a moderate Peronist) took office with CFK as Vice President. Facing major foreign indebtedness, his first task was to rearrange Argentina's payment schedule, which was impossible to meet for the country's economy. Furthermore, the crisis worsened due to economic stagnation stemming from the COVID-19 pandemic. At press time, Fernández was navigating through his first year in office, having successfully renegotiated the debt with foreign creditors, but failing to present an economic plan for Argentinians to see the light at the end of the tunnel in terms of economic stability.

In the past, Alberto Fernández – who served as Chief of Staff during Kirchner's administration – was able to keep in good terms with Grupo Clarín. His administration's media policies did not introduce major innovations other than declaring connectivity services a public service. To this day, regulation on how the decree introducing this legislation will be enforced – a regulation that has been fiercely criticized by Grupo Clarín – is still pending.

Notes

1 In 1949, the government drew up a new Constitution that allowed for presidential reelection, which was later repealed in 1955. Presidential terms were six years long. Since 1994, reelection was once again permitted, but terms were shortened to four years.
2 Until 1978, Argentina did not produce newsprint paper and had to acquire the material abroad. The situation was aggravated by a constant lack of currency.
3 Raúl Lastiri served as Argentine president for just a few months, between Cámpora's resignation and Perón's election to office.
4 Center party that had governed the country between 1916 and 1930, and 1963 and 1966.
5 By an act of Congress, the value of the Argentine peso was directly tied to the US dollar (1 peso = 1 dollar).

References

Basualdo, Eduardo (2001). *Sistema político y modelo de acumulación en la Argentina*. Bernal: Universidad Nacional de Quilmes.
Basualdo, Eduardo (2010). *Estudios de historia económica argentina*. Buenos Aires: Siglo XXI.
Becerra, Martín (2016). *Restauración*. https://martinbecerra.wordpress.com/2016/01/14/restauracion/

Gerchunoff, Pablo and Lucas Llach (1998). *El ciclo de la ilusión y el desencanto. Un siglo de políticas económicas argentinas.* Buenos Aires: Emecé.

O'Donnell, Guillermo (1982). *El Estado Burocrático Autoritario.* Buenos Aires: Editorial de Belgrano.

Nun, José (2010). "Sobre el concepto de masa marginal". In *Lavboratorio. Revista de estudios sobre cambio estructural y desigualdad.* No. 23.

Portantiero, Juan Carlos (1989). "Economía y política en la crisis argentina". In Ansaldi, W. and Moreno, J. (eds.). *Estado y sociedad en el pensamiento nacional,* pp. 320–338. Buenos Aires: Cántaro.

Rossi, Diego (2008). "La radiodifusión entre 1990-1995: exacerbación del modelo privado-comercial", in En M. Guillermo (ed.). *Mucho Ruido y pocas leyes. Economía y políticas de comunicación en la Argentina* (2nd ed., pp. 239–260). Buenos Aires: La Crujía.

Varela, Mirta (2005). *La televisión criolla.* Buenos Aires: Edhasa.

2 Politics under the Skin

A Wake-Up Call (1945–1958)

The history of Clarín, as a newspaper first and as a business conglomerate later, is inseparable from the vicissitudes that Argentine politics has experienced since 1945. The last 75 years of political developments in the country were as intense as they were varied, with governments of various political colors and a wide range of ideological orientations (even when presidents belonged to the same party). Furthermore, the period included 18 years under dictatorial governments that came to power through coups, the last of which was especially bloody. With all of them, Grupo Clarín did business and obtained benefits, except for the two terms of Cristina Fernández de Kirchner (CFK) (12/2007–12/2011; 12/2011–12/2015). And with almost all of them the company also had conflicts of varying magnitude and impact on its projection as a leader of the media system, a media system in which the political negotiation of journalistic companies with governments is routine both in Argentina and in the rest of Latin America. This practice is a precondition for accessing and maintaining licenses, official advertising, tax relief or tax exemptions, exclusive contents and other vital inputs for the sector's economy. Politics can be thought of as a tattoo on the skin of the main communication group in Argentina.

The imprints of Roberto Noble, the Group's founder and director until his death in 1969, and of his successors, reinforce the role of Grupo Clarín as a "political actor," which in Borrat's (1989) opinion fits the description of every newspaper. In this case, aligned with the tradition of Argentine newspapers since the 19th century, *Clarín*'s motivation and action in the political sphere are evident from its very inception.

Noble had been a national deputy for the Independent Socialist Party in the early1930s. He was an advocate for Intellectual Property

Law No. 11723, which was still in force in Argentina at the end of 2020, and, later on, held the position of Minister of Government – the main role within the cabinet – for the Buenos Aires Province administration of Manuel Fresco, a conservative with Nazi-fascist inclinations (1936 to 1939). Noble withdrew from professional politics, accused of irregularities in the management of public funds during the following years. In 1945, he returned to the public arena with the creation of *Clarín*.

The foundation of the newspaper received financial support that was never acknowledged but has been documented by Sivak (2013), for instance, from the German Embassy in the aftermath of the Nazi regime. In a way, starting the newspaper was a confirmation of Noble's withdrawal from the big leagues of the political and electoral competition, with a new undertaking: To exert influence through his "wake-up call," as the foundational slogan of the newspaper claimed.[1] Just as Bartolomé Mitre, the founder of *La Nación*, another leading newspaper in the country and partner of *Clarín* since 1977, Noble chose to continue attracting the attention of the public and building a mass audience to keep alive his ideology in the political debate – not from a partisan perspective but through the factory of news and opinions: The newsroom.

As an editor consciously seeking to be involved in public policy from the pages of the newspaper, Noble can be regarded as part of the tradition of José C. Paz (*La Prensa*), Mitre (*La Nación*) and Natalio Botana (*Crítica*), among other famous creators of newspapers of great social, political and economic influence in Argentina. In the following decades, other popular experiences focusing on mass audiences followed the same path, such as the publication introduced by Héctor Ricardo García (*Crónica*). And yet there were other cases that did not become as massive but were no less outstanding in the field of political journalism, with influential opinions shaping the public agenda, including opinion leaders Jacobo Timerman (*La Opinión*), Julio Ramos (*Ámbito Financiero*) or Jorge Lanata (*Página 12*).

A light and casual style characterized *Clarín* from its beginnings, with a tabloid format unlike most of the newspapers of the time, which were broadsheet in size. The front page was designed with catchy headlines that invited readers to the articles inside, a layout that set it apart from the other Argentine dailies, which until then displayed part of the articles on the front page.

Despite having supported the Democratic Union in the 1946 elections, in tune with the majority of the media, *Clarín* was one of the first to recognize the legitimacy of Juan Perón's electoral victory and nurtured good relations with his first two administrations. Compared to the openly hostile editorial line of market leading papers such as *La Prensa* and *La Nación*, Noble and his editorial staff were sympathetic to an administration that in its economic policy had direct points of contact with the incipient developmentalism that Noble was to embrace over the following years. *Clarín* benefited from the expropriation of *La Prensa* in 1951 ordered by Congress as part of an official initiative to control newspapers and radio stations; the transfer of *La Prensa* to the General Labor Confederation (CGT), which caused a migration of readers; and, above all, the neglect of classified ads, which *Clarín* captured by offering promotional prices for massive advertisers. The newspaper gradually grew in terms of both readership and influence. Noble maintained contact with, requested state aid of and obtained benefits from the press and communication department of the Perón governments, in such matters as the management of paper import quotas, among others.

The foundations of *Clarín* in its early years included the transfer of middle-class readers from *La Prensa* to *Clarín*; the formation of a newsroom with key figures from Botana's mythical *Crítica*; Noble's securing of paper import quotas; and the political editorial line without critiques that would have placed his newspaper on the radar of government control, while some of its competitors were eroded by either frontal disputes against or open submission to Perón. In addition, thanks to Noble's good contacts with the government, as reported by his numerous and affectionate telegrams to Perón's Undersecretary of Press and Communication, Raúl Apold, *Clarín* secured permission to use the *Crítica* workshops for printing its copies at a price that Botana's family considered unfair.

The reading of the political, social and economic situation during the second Perón administration and the climate of opposition prevailing in the urban middle classes, coupled with rifts with the government over the supply of paper, led *Clarín* to support the coup d'état of 1955. It was the start of a series of headlines and editorial positions ranging from indulgence to explicit celebration of all the military risings and the overthrowing of constitutional governments that ensued. The events led to the removal from office in the following years of Arturo Frondizi (he was removed in 1962, possibly the only case in which there was neither indulgence nor celebration, but rather a failure to react faced with the ousting of an ally), Arturo Illia (he was removed in 1966) and María Estela Martínez de Perón (she was removed in 1976). The formula that Noble applied to the paper, as Sivak described, was based on "his ideological flexibility, his skills as a political negotiator, his ability to capture period climates, and his desire for social advancement" (2013: 27).

With the dictatorship of the self-proclaimed "Liberating Revolution" (1955–1958), *Clarín*'s editorials backed the military government from the beginning, overacting its anti-Peronism to the point of calling Perón a dictator and portraying the paper as another "victim" of the injuries caused by Perón's rule against freedom of the press. Noble also sought to preserve, with dictator Aramburu, the businesses that depended on government discretion, such as the permission to use the *Crítica* workshops to print *Clarín* newspapers.

The Developmentalist Platform (1958–1976)

After Arturo Frondizi was elected in 1958 (with Peronism banned from the elections),[2] the newspaper openly demonstrated that it welcomed the developmentalist socio-economic model conveyed by Frondizi and, in particular, his strongest champion, Rogelio Frigerio. Noble died in 1969 and his "ideological, political and financial" alliance (Borrelli and Saborido, 2013) with those leaders was so powerful that when his partner, Ernestina Herrera, whom he had married when his illness was already advanced, was left in charge of the daily; she was tutored and assisted by them in the editorial room. Indeed, this link actively appeared

> in the paper's editorial line of thinking and in the participation of developmentalists in the newsroom, who exercised a true 'ideological control' of the editorial line. For *Clarín* and developmentalism, the economy was the basis on which all the other levels of Argentine social life depended. Without taking the 'great leap' from underdevelopment to the development that would re-found Argentine society, the pressing national problems could not be solved.
> (Borrelli and Saborido, 2013: 202)

Frondizi found in Noble a firm ally who, without engaging in militant journalism, defended each of the main lines of government. For his part, Noble had a daily relationship with the president and his closest collaborators, which allowed him to exert influence and to benefit from the credit lines of Banco Nación, to obtain aid for the importation of paper and income from official advertising. Moreover, President Frondizi helped in the purchase of the land and in the construction of the building that *Clarín* has occupied in the Constitución neighborhood since 1960. The government's favoritism toward *Clarín* elicited complaints from its competitors (Sivak, 2013: 139 and subsequent pages).

The mass scale of the newspaper accelerated in the 1960s in line with the diversification and growth of cultural industries such as cinema, private TV stations and book publishing (with the boom in Latin American literature and emblems such as the publishing house of the University of Buenos Aires, Eudeba, which published books on social and human sciences with broad circulation). In a decade agitated by revolts and revolutions all over the planet, especially in the Third World, the sixties were years of relative economic well-being in Argentina, but hectic institutional activity, since there were new coups or disruptions of constitutional regimes. The only two presidents who were elected while the electoral majority was banned were Frondizi and Arturo Illia, and they both had to leave office de facto. On top of the banning of Peronism, a left-wing political culture emerged, which found the Cuban Revolution to be a model and a reason to feed the internal debate. In parallel, conflict with the unions mounted in a country where the labor movement had high levels of organization. In this context, *Clarín* brought some intellectual figures from the left wing and from Peronism into the newsroom, while witnessing the appearance of new journalistic companies with which it would share the media environment of the time, such as the newspaper *Crónica*, created by Héctor Ricardo García (1963), and the magazines *Primera Plana* (1962) and *Confirmado* (1965), founded by Jacobo Timerman, who had served as a columnist for *Clarín* between 1958 and 1959.

Clarín was critical of the weak presidency of Illia, who belonged to the traditional faction of the Radical Party (UCR Party), and was strongly favorable to the developmentalist branch of the Radical Party proposed by Frondizi, with whom Noble met periodically. In those years, a representative of the developmentalist cadres, Oscar Camilion,[3] was anointed secretary general of the newspaper's editorial office, a position he held between 1965 and 1972. The influence on the newspaper exerted by representatives of Frondizi's faction increased until 1981.

Noble died at the beginning of 1969 during the dictatorship that had started in 1966 with the coup d'état of Juan Carlos Onganía, a government that Noble supported. Two years before, he had married young Ernestina Herrera, which was not easy because Noble had been married before and had a biological daughter (Guadalupe Noble Zapata) with his first wife. Herrera de Noble stayed at the newspaper, formally as its director until her passing in 2017. She had eventually settled inheritance matters with Guadalupe, and relied on the developmentalist cadres surrounding Frigerio for the day-to-day operation of the company, the direction of the newsroom and the planning of new paths for *Clarín*.

Noble's succession was not easy, especially due to struggles in the newspaper's newsroom; however, Frigerism had been identified by the paper's founder as an ideological and administrative guardian of the company and Noble's widow found relief in that core of lucid and pragmatic men, entrusting them with gigantic tasks for which she was not qualified. Starting with Camilion, followed by Octavio Frigerio, Carlos Zaffore and Enrique Durruty, they all took turns at the paper's editorial lead.

In 1972, Rogelio Frigerio brought young developmentalist Héctor Magnetto onboard in the administrative management of the newspaper. Magnetto had studied accounting at the National University of La Plata and was called in to straighten out a complicated financial and economic situation. It was a stormy time for the country, and *Clarín*, with a politicized newsroom, suffered the consequences of mismanagement, disputes over Noble's inheritance and attempts by sectors of Peronism to share quotas of power with the developmentalists who surrounded Ernestina and ran the business. The newspaper's lawyer and Frigerio's partner, Bernardo Sofovich, was kidnapped by a branch of *Ejército Revolucionario del Pueblo* (People's Revolutionary Army, ERP), called ERP-August 22, which, as a condition of his release, required the publication of an advertorial that deteriorated relations between the paper's leadership and Perón on the eve of the inauguration to his third (brief) presidency.

After Perón's death on July 1, 1974, *Clarín* accepted for the first time a government delegate of sorts in the editorial office, as a peace offering to a government with which it had experienced friction and with whose Minister of Economy, José Ber Gelbard, Frigerio had personal and political discrepancies. The experiment was short-lived and not very fruitful for any of the parties involved.

At that time, journalism suffered open government censorship, and many professionals were persecuted by the state repression mechanisms of the security forces and the parastatal *Alianza Anticomunista Argentina* (dubbed "Triple A").

Similar to the rest of the media, *Clarín*'s history up to 1983 was contemporaneous with more or less intense cycles of public censorship under all governments (taking into consideration that the electoral ban on Peronism as of 1955 was a clear form of censorship and that the first two Perón administrations showed repeated censoring actions as well). In the 1970s, the only censorship-free period was the brief presidency of Héctor Cámpora (from 05/25/1973 to 07/13/1973). However, the censoring cycle was reinstated after his resignation, and formalized in 1974 with Law 20840, which provided penalties of two to six years in prison "to anyone disseminating, advertising or distributing news altering or suppressing institutional order and social peace of the Nation". Explicit censorship escalated incessantly and unprecedentedly after the coup d'état of March 24, 1976.

Dictatorship and Deals (1976–1983)

Like its media counterparts, *Clarín* had to cope with censorship and negotiate the conditions of enunciation and statement of news and opinions, i.e. explore the limits of what could be said. Although existing in varying degrees during most of the first four decades of the paper's existence, these conditions were present and framed the relations with the various governments. Similar to all other journalistic companies in the country, *Clarín* needed to cooperate. The media system had to develop the ability to live with censorship, which was a constant in Argentine politics until 1983, albeit with brief exceptions. Thus it would be unfair to say that *Clarín* suffered more than other newspapers. Nor can it be argued that censorship determined the main lines of the paper's editorial positioning. Support for the coup of the Military Junta of Jorge Videla, Emilio Massera and Orlando Agosti ushered in a period of adherence that would only find political overtones after Argentina's defeat in the Malvinas/Falklands War (1982). Prior to that time, the paper restricted its criticism of the dictatorial government to disapproval of economic matters only.

The combination of repression at the political, cultural and intellectual level, on the one hand, and a significant retraction of the purchasing power of workers, i.e. the target audience for the cultural industries, on the other hand, brought about a radical restructuring of the media system and related activities.

By proposing the drastic disarticulation of the compensatory policies for social, economic and cultural inequalities, which policies were based on consensus and determined the conflict over the political and cultural leadership of society, the coup d'état of 1976 required exerting direct repression of both a massive and an individualized nature, and instilling terror as a strategy for social discipline. The adherence of *Clarín*'s leadership to this dictatorial plan and to its method of state terrorism concurred with the militant support provided by *La Nación*, *La Prensa* or *La Razón*, and even by newspapers with less conservative lines, such as *La Opinion* or *Crónica*.

The decline in consumption of publications (newspapers, periodicals and books) during that period was gradually offset by increased consumption of radio and TV, two media types presumed to be free access. Between 1970 and 1980, more than 250 newspapers closed, thus eroding the diversity of the press. The shift in mass information/entertainment consumption from print to audiovisual media facilitated the control of messages, as audiovisual media outlets were in the hands of the state after the military forces took them by assault, splitting the administration of channels based in the capital city, Buenos Aires, between the Army, Navy and Air Force (reserving *Canal 7* for the Executive). However, *Clarín* did very well and grew in sales during this time.

The main newspapers that had stimulated the pro-coup social atmosphere were rewarded in 1976 by the military government with shares of the only newsprint factory in the country, Papel Prensa.[4] The Videla administration forced the successors of its shareholder David Graiver (who died in a mysterious plane crash) to transfer the company to a consortium formed by the newspapers *Clarín, La Razón, La Nación* and the National State. This maneuver was described as "one of the most serious corruption cases in Argentine history," since it "revealed the relationships and procedures used by the large power groups," according to former National Prosecutor for Administrative Investigations Ricardo Molinas (Molinas & Molinas, 1993).

Thus, the leadership of the newspaper Clarín managed to partner with the state, *La Nación* and *La Razón*, in dispossessing the shares of Papel Prensa from Graiver's relatives, which his widow, Lidia Papaleo, denounced as an act of pressure agreed upon by the dictatorship and the owners of the journalistic companies. Graciela Mochkofsky (2011) reports confirmation of the events reported by Papaleo, by one of Videla's spokesmen. With this move, *Clarín* managed to access the key raw material for an industry that would still enjoy at least two decades of splendor, social influence, massive reach and good business, before the contraction caused by the impact of the digital revolution, which began to be felt in Argentina at the turn of the century.

Furthermore, the extraordinary partnership between the dictatorial state and private media in the paper mill, the critical resource for the newspaper market, illustrates the change in the model of state intervention instituted by the military regime. The echoes of the Papel Prensa case still resonate today, given that the transfer of assets initiated with collective contributions for the benefit of a handful of actors can be viewed as a process of original accumulation by concentrated capital ownership in a peculiar joint venture with the state. For *Clarín*, the involvement in Papel Prensa was the starting point for a process of expansion toward other activities that never stopped, and encompassed not only the media but other sectors of the economy, as well. Quid pro quo: The editorials and the political section of *Clarín* thanked and extolled the dictatorial rule. On the first anniversary of the coup, for example, the newspaper praised a "genuinely democratic power, sensitive to the interests and aspirations of the masses." In the glum years of state terror, Clarín refused to publish habeas corpus petitions and claims of the relatives of kidnapped and missing people, rejecting the publication of complaints pointing to massive human rights violations.

Until the final stretch of the dictatorship, the main private media outlets did not differ in their editorial line from the official messages propagated by radio and television stations that were mostly under state control. The media acted as those consensus-building artifacts that reinforced the repressive domination of the military government. *Clarín* was no exception. However, as documented in the doctoral thesis of Marcelo Borrelli (2011), the leadership of the newspaper opted for an economic model that differed from the one defined by the Military Junta, as the latter, far from accepting any developmental principle, was a detractor of the import substitution industrialization process that characterized the country's productive structure, and encouraged the model of agricultural export of raw materials and financial valuation.

Within *Clarín*, a line of enthusiastic political support for the dictatorship coexisted with a persistent criticism of its economic plan from the perspective of Frondizi-Frigerio style developmentalism. This coexistence was not peaceful, and the old guard was expelled in 1981. It was a milestone: Magnetto, the man who had run the *Clarín* administration in the previous decade with unswerving determination as he ordered massive layoffs among other cost-cutting measures, took over the company's management together with Ernestina Herrera, and became a shareholder. Dismissing those who had accompanied Noble in his early journey was no easy task for the widow of *Clarín*'s founder. With the guidance offered by Frigerio and his entourage, she had managed to put the company back on track and even modify her private life. In the first year of the dictatorship, she had adopted two children, Marcela and Felipe, in irregular conditions arranged by the old developmentalist core.[5] These irregular adoptions led to four-decade-long claims based on suspicions that they could be the children of missing people who had been kidnapped during the dictatorship.

After having praised the peace and order imposed by the dictatorship in its editorials, rejecting complaints about human rights violations or the suspension of constitutional guarantees and freedoms, *Clarín* joined the efforts to demand elections. Such efforts started to multiply in the country after Argentina's defeat in the Malvinas/

Falklands War, while human rights organizations, unions and political parties began to mobilize.

Democracy and Multimedia Expansion (1983–2002)

With that turn, not carried out in isolation, *Clarín* gave its support to the democratic agenda that reinstated the constitutional regime in 1983, when Raúl Alfonsín (UCR Party) won the presidential elections – although the paper showed greater preference for the candidate who was defeated, Peronism's Ítalo Luder. The return to democracy was followed by the Trial of the Military Juntas in 1985. Both milestones constituted learning opportunities for the media system. At the end of the dictatorial regime, *Clarín* was the leading newspaper in terms of sales, contrasted with the steady decline of *Crónica*, the paper that had the highest circulation before the coup d'état. This was partly explained because the latter's readership was the working class, a sector that was beaten down as never before by the economic failure brought about by the dictatorship.

Argentina was setting in motion an unmatched process of conquering the right to freedom of expression and the eradication of censorship, with some actors clearly more favorably positioned than others in terms of resources to take advantage of the new situation. By 1983, *Clarín* was not only the most significant newspaper in the market, but it was also a partner in Papel Prensa company, and one of the main shareholders of the DyN (*Diarios y Noticias*) News Agency,[6] which had been founded on the eve of the Argentine landing on the Malvinas/ Falkland Islands in March 1982, in partnership with *La Nación, La Gaceta, Río Negro* and other newspapers in the country. That germ of business diversification, undertaken at the beginning of Magnetto's reign, accelerated with his leadership in the following decades.

Under the Alfonsín administration, *Clarín* succeeded in taking control of *Radio Mitre* through third parties. *Radio Mitre* was (and still is) one of Argentina's main stations, both in its AM (*Radio Mitre*) and in its FM (*100*) versions. However, the transaction was only formalized under the Carlos Menem administration in 1989. Although the paper had supported the social mood of the "democratic spring" of Alfonsín's early years, Alfonsín's reluctance to facilitate the expansion of *Clarín* to the radio broadcasting segment,[7] as Magnetto intended, represented a point of conflict – it was reflected in critical editorial coverage against the government, and evidenced in the president's speeches, in which he questioned *Clarín*'s bias against his administration.

In the last stretch of Alfonsín's presidency, the economic crisis that culminated in hyperinflation represented the divorce with the government of a growing part of the electorate, which was accompanied by *Clarín's* critical coverage. One of the most controversial episodes was the uprising of the *carapintada* military insurgents who undermined the constitutional order and found favorable treatment in *Clarín's* front pages and editorials. The Clarín leadership held "political" meetings with some of their leaders (Sivak, 2013), which became testimony of the Magnetto's pressure against an administration. This remains in the memory of the Radical Party leaders of these years. *Clarín* took on the role of interpreter and spokesperson for the extended middle class and conveyed its moods, sympathies and rancor. The political pressures of its editorial leadership against the government were not publicly condemned by the government except on rare occasions, such as a memorable speech by Alfonsín in which he identified *Clarín* as a "staunch opponent" in 1987, after enduring editorial attacks from the paper. The middle-class sectors who read *Clarín* for the most part favored the UCR Party in the elections until 1987, when Peronism introduced a set of referents aligned behind a renovated agenda, winning the approval not only of the working class, but also of the broad middle layers of society.

With the decline of the Alfonsín administration came a turn in Peronism, which won the elections with its candidate Carlos Menem, governor of La Rioja Province, who had defeated the up-and-coming governor of Buenos Aires Province, Antonio Cafiero, in the party elections. After winning the presidential contest in 1989 with promises of salary improvements and inclusion, Menem deployed an aggressive privatization program, instrumented through processes that were tainted with accusations of corruption. Alfonsín negotiated the early handover of command with Menem amid hyperinflation and social and business protests that persisted in the following years, as *Clarín's* expansive efforts accelerated.

Only five months into his inauguration, Menem granted the license of a leading television station in Buenos Aires, *Canal 13*, to Grupo Clarín. Prior to that, during the Menem administration, Congress had passed one of the laws that served as a pillar for the privatizations of the 1990s, State Reform Law No. 23696, which modified one of the articles of the Broadcasting Decree (22285 of 1980) in force, which prohibited cross-ownership between print and audiovisual media. Thus, Grupo Clarín landed on *Canal 13*, and so did Editorial Atlántida with *Telefé*. The new legislation facilitated not only the creation of multimedia groups, but also the privatization of utilities – telephones, railways, electricity, gas and water companies – and the handing over of state assets, such as the oil and gas company YPF, to the private sector.

In the following years, Grupo Clarín consolidated its position in the audiovisual market by formalizing its ownership of *Radio Mitre / FM 100*, which it was already controlling. Furthermore, the Group developed, in competition with other companies, its expansion toward the cable TV market (Marino, 2013). The signing of a contract for exclusive screening rights between the Argentine Soccer Association (AFA) and the company Torneos, owned by Carlos Ávila, was a catapult for household subscriptions to cable TV with additional benefits – such as a grid in which the free-to-air channels streamed without interference, and cinema channels that had no advertising breaks, among others.

President Menem claimed that Grupo Clarín did not show explicit support in return for the benefits obtained in the first months of his first term and the relationship between the government and Grupo Clarín became strained. In the meantime, the group of companies led by Magnetto expanded its dominance of the pay TV market, first in the metropolitan area of Buenos Aires and later on in the rest of the country with the Multicanal brand. The 1994 Constitutional Reform allowed for presidential reelection (Menem was reelected in 1995) and, by giving constitutional status to international treaties ratified by Congress, allowed the entry of US capital into the media sector.

During Menem's second term, the sector was shaped by three factors: Concentration, financierization of property and the arrival of foreign capital in media ownership. *Clarín* formalized its expansive process by publicly recognizing itself as Grupo Clarín and emphasizing – with great publicity – its national character. However, to acquire small cable companies, it allowed a minority stake by a US company (Goldman Sachs), while taking loans abroad in a macroeconomic framework characterized by the parity between the national currency (peso) and the US dollar.

In the last years of the Menem administration, a rival of Clarín emerged with notable strength. Telefónica, a subsidiary of Telefónica Spain, inherited a multimedia arrangement, initially aligned with the ruling party, made up of broadcast TV channels and radio stations, in addition to being the incumbent telephone carrier for the southern half of the country (the incumbent in the northern half was Telecom Argentina). Telefónica became the owner of the main free-to-air TV network, *Telefé*, until its sale to the Viacom Group in 2016. While Grupo Clarín had a commitment to cable TV, a segment where Telefónica was not present, the telco was focused on an area in which Grupo

Clarín had only made a fleeting attempt with CTI Móvil; therefore, the only area of competition between the two conglomerates was actually the free-to-air TV segment.

At the turn of the century, Grupo Clarín experienced a shift in its income pattern. Until the end of the 1990s, the revenues of the multimedia group depended mainly on the production of journalistic and fictional content. At the beginning of the 21st century, a new business unit became the most profitable segment (Sivak, 2015): Cable TV and connectivity services associated with the Multicanal network, especially after the third largest cable operator in the country, VCC, sold its subscriber base 50-50 to Cablevisión and Multicanal, and the massive cable TV market ended up concentrated in a few hands. In the same decade, Clarín consolidated its dominance of the main audiovisual market, and obtained from the first head of government of the City of Buenos Aires to be elected by citizens, Fernando de la Rúa (UCR Party), an exemption to the requirement to bury the cables for its network, which not only facilitated its expansion but was anticompetitive, as other companies did not enjoy the same benefit.

The organizational structure of the conglomerate has had influence over its content. As its "infotainment" (information/entertainment) units lost relevance and its connectivity and telecom networks gained momentum over the last two decades, Grupo Clarín's behavior has shown two trends: On the one hand, the Group's media culture was subservient to the expansion of its telecom and connectivity businesses and, on the other hand, the consolidation of these businesses served as a stepping stone to reach the pinnacle of economic power in the country.

The heritage of the fertileculture of the media was subordinated to the corporate strategy of survival (2002–2003), expansion (until 2008) and, after that, an open war against Kirchnerism (after 2008), both when CFK was president (2007–2015) and when – with a contrary strategy and stimulating the unprecedented expansion of Grupo Clarín – Macri was president (2015–2019), with the militant support of Grupo Clarín in a strategy of "opposing the opposition" of Macri (i.e. Kirchnerism), and even when Alberto Fernández became president (2019).

The change in the Group's income pattern gave birth to a new paradigm in which the journalistic companies would gradually lose influence and relative participation in the decision-making landscape of the conglomerate's leadership. The failure of the presidency of Fernando de la Rúa – which Clarín supported as much as it pressured to limit the power of Telefónica – and the institutional, economic and social crisis that his fall and the interim presidency of Eduardo Duhalde represented (2002–May 2003) activated an unprecedented battery of lobbying resources in Grupo Clarín and other media and communications groups. Indeed, the discontinuation of the peso-dollar convertibility put many companies on the brink of bankruptcy due to the impossibility of meeting their commitments with their external creditors after sustained indebtedness in the previous decade. Duhalde attenuated the effects of the devaluation in the media companies, and Grupo Clarín made a memorable attempt to exonerate the interim president in its depiction of a major piece of news. When two social activists ("picketers") were murdered in a massive protest in June 2002, despite having a photographic record documenting that they had been killed in a cold-blooded execution by Buenos Aires Police officers, *Clarín* used the headline "The crisis has caused two new deaths," adding that it was not known who had shot them. Until then, Duhalde had not set a date for the elections – that is, for the end of his interim term – and the case, known as the "Avellaneda Massacre," forced the call for elections to be formalized in March 2003.

Defensive Concentration (2002–2008)

The March 2003 elections yielded a very close result: Menem was the candidate with the most votes, with 24.3 percent, and Néstor Kirchner came second, with 22 percent. Menem stepped down from the ballot and Kirchner assumed the presidency in May in a condition of political weakness.

Grupo Clarín's defensive concentration process had a series of hallmarks: The negotiation of state relief that materialized in the enactment of the Law for the Preservation of Cultural Assets – negotiated by Duhalde and approved in the first weeks of Kirchner's term in June 2003 – and subsequently in the renewal of radio and television licenses, in the deferment of audiovisual licenses for ten years (Necessity and Urgency Decree No. 527/2005) and finally in the approval of the merger of Multicanal and Cablevisión throughout Kirchner's mandate. Thus, the Group managed to restructure its private debt with external creditors, consolidate its large participation in all segments of the media industry and in 2007 expand its dominance in the most lucrative of all these businesses, cable TV.

The original weak legitimacy of Kirchner's tenure was countered by a program of action that was transgressive in several aspects. The recomposition of state authority through the appointment of a Supreme Court of Justice independent from the government, the promotion of trials for human rights violations, the reopening of joint negotiations with unions (fundamentally, but not only, about wages) and the macroeconomic recovery were all measures that built social and political support for the president. But this justification for the significant measures adopted by Kirchner promoting the concentration of the media system and the alliance with Grupo Clarín and other media conglomerates does not suffice to explain why, after the presidential elections of 2007, when Cristina Fernández was elected with an advantage of more than 20 points over her adversaries – i.e. with a landslide electoral legitimacy and political capital – Kirchner authorized the merger between Cablevisión and Multicanal (Grupo Clarín) on his last day in office.

During Kirchner's presidency, the editorial line of the Group's numerous media outlets was supportive of the actions of the governments, which, in addition to good business, offered a large number of on- and off-the-record scoops to *Clarín*'s most notorious chief editors, columnists and opinion-makers.

When Kirchner became president in 2003, the media system had undergone a major transformation and modernization, but was bankrupt. The sector had been concentrated in only a few groups, national and foreign, some of them associated with financial capital. The concentration was of a conglomerate nature, that is to say, the groups in many cases went beyond their initial businesses and had expanded to other media segments (multimedia) as well as to other industries, which meant that in several markets there were dominant actors. The productive sector had gone through a technology upgrade. The organization of the creation and editing processes had mutated due to the outsourcing of content production, which, in turn, had stimulated a dynamic base of production companies of different sizes. Furthermore, new aesthetic patterns had been forged both in television fiction and in journalistic genres; the film industry had been resurrected by the Film Law of 1994 (see Marino, 2013); and the centralization of production in Buenos Aires had increased, a trend that Menem legalized in his second term through an authorization for the operation of radio and television networks.

The 2001 crisis had caused a significant retraction in subscriber-based segments of cultural industries (with drops in cable television subscriptions, and in the purchase of newspapers, magazines, books and records and movie tickets), dramatically reducing advertising investment and, consequently, disrupting the entire system. The Kirchner presidency – whose Chief of Staff was Alberto Fernández, who became president in late 2019 – gave support to the inherited media structure through stimulus policies. It conceived a state aid scheme in exchange for editorial support, encouraged improvements in the programming of *Canal 7*, and its media policy became aligned with the most important players in the sector, while affirming its alliance in the telecom field with the dominant carriers (Becerra, 2015). In addition, Kirchner created the cultural TV channel *Encuentro* in the orbit of the Ministry of Education – a groundbreaking measure in the history of Argentine state-run TV, since it raised the quality standards of productions to unprecedented levels.

During the Néstor Kirchner administration, the media in general and the audiovisual sector in particular were economically rebuilt, and experienced a rebirth of content and format exports, gaining momentum due to the competitiveness of the exchange rate.

As other presidents in Latin America, each in their own way, Kirchner exercised a presidential style of political communication that did away with the intermediation of journalists when communicating news or stating a position on issues of the public agenda. This style of direct communication studied by Rincón (2010) annoyed many journalists and presenters, especially the most prestigious ones, who were used to receiving deferential treatment from the highest state authorities. Furthermore, Kirchner did not hold press conferences and gave very few interviews. However, it is necessary to draw a difference between the changes in style of presidential political communications and media policymaking. In this case, the first of the three terms of the Kirchnerist cycle did not promote major changes in the industry, and coexisted with the main shareholders of the large groups, which included more than a dozen private encounters with Magnetto. As Sivak reflects in the second volume of his detailed history of *Clarín* ("The Magnetto era"), Kirchner and Magnetto had the same public, which constituted a political base for the former, and an audience for the latter.

On his last business day in office (12/07/2007), Kirchner authorized the merger between Cablevisión and Multicanal. To grasp the economic importance of this merger, it suffices to say that the absorbed company (Cablevisión) contributed more than 70 percent of the income to the Group's accounts in 2010. In return for the favors received during the Néstor Kirchner administration, Grupo Clarín was particularly deferential in its editorials, showing only mild criticism and nimble support for the ruling party.

War against CFK (2008–2015)

The mutually beneficial relationship between Kirchnerism and Grupo Clarín shattered at the beginning of the first CFK administration. Indeed, soon after CFK's inauguration in December 2007, the so-called "crisis of the countryside"[8] occurred in March 2008. This became a milestone in the political and social polarization for at least the following 12 years, the time frame during which a conflict erupted between the government and Grupo Clarín, the main multimedia corporation.

Since 2008, the government began to act against some of the Group's interests, in some cases on behalf of the social interest (as with the Audiovisual Media Law) and in others forgetting about society and exhibiting its clumsiest and most overstated attitudes, as in the much publicized inspection of hundreds of auditors of the Tax Authority (AFIP) at the Group's headquarters. Grupo Clarín, for its part, responded with a media arsenal that had not been seen in Argentine journalism since Illia's time, including the blatant change of position of its main presenters and columnists, who until 2008 had been indulgent with the Kirchners and suddenly turned into bitter opponents.

In January 2010, Néstor Kirchner, in an interview with journalist Horacio Verbitsky on *Página 12*, attempted to explain the dispute with Grupo Clarín as a result of the corporate voracity of a group that had exerted pressure on him for the purpose of taking over Telecom. The explanation was as plausible as it was unsatisfactory: If Kirchner as president had agreed to Grupo Clarín's corporate demands during his administration, if he amicably chatted with Magnetto at the presidential residence, what difference did Telecom make?

What happened from 2008 on was a warlike escalation between Grupo Clarín and Kirchnerism that has not stopped. During the CFK administrations, part of the conflict was promoted by policy-making in the field of communications (comprising the media sector and telecommunications) that were unprecedented in Argentine history for their intensity and for the prominence that, based on the government's initiative, they had in the public space. Although formally these initiatives did not only involve Clarín, because it was the largest concentrated multimedia and the most powerful political actor in the infocommunication sector, they significantly affected it.

The political agenda presided over by the controversy between Kirchnerism and Grupo Clarín was accentuated by a polarization of the journalistic field that gave rise to the emergence of figures of "militant journalism" (identified with Kirchnerism) that condemned the most traditional (and clearly ideologically anti-Kirchner) notion of "independent journalism." The journalistic companies took sides, depending on whether they were supporters or detractors of the two opposing poles.

The Papel Prensa case (Mochkofsky, 2011), the questioning of the Fibertel case, the creation of the *Fútbol Para Todos*[9] program, the adoption of the Japanese-Brazilian standard for digital terrestrial television in a plan that initially aspired to take subscribers away from cable TV and the enactment of Audiovisual Communication Services Law No. 26522 in October 2009 are manifestations of the media policy carried out by the two CFK administrations in the heat of the conflict with Grupo Clarín. This list would be incomplete without mentioning the increase in funding granted to those media outlets that were supportive of the government, using public resources in the form of official advertising at significant levels. Those levels became slightly more moderate during the Macri presidency, and Alberto Fernández continued to attenuate them.

CFK also complied with the decriminalization of the offenses of slander and perjury in cases of public interest that the Inter-American Court of Human Rights demanded of Argentina, which meant an important regulatory advance for the right to freedom of expression.

In the second year of CFK's first term, Congress approved, for the second time in Argentine history, a law on radio and television (the first had been in 1953; the rest of the comprehensive regulations for the sector were established by military governments): Audiovisual Communication Services Law No. 26522, which was resisted by Grupo Clarín and other commercial media conglomerates. Grupo Clarín not only actively campaigned against the social and parliamentary discussion of the law, but after it was approved, Grupo Clarín also brought a legal case against it. The case was deferred with filings of precautionary measures and delays, and four years later, the Supreme Court of Justice issued a famous ruling in favor of the state. In 2013, only one of the seven magistrates of the highest court validated the arguments of Magnetto's Group, which suffered an unexpected setback (Mastrini and Becerra, 2017).

The strategy defined by the CFK administration to force Grupo Clarín to conform to the audiovisual law, contrasted with less stringent demands on other conglomerates like Telefónica (then owner of the largest open TV network, *Telefé*), was to take de-concentration back to the courts as one of the main objectives of the regulation passed by Congress in 2009. This new phase of litigation occurred at the end of the second CFK administration, and – as was foreseeable – the main multimedia group ultimately did not conform. The regulatory change decreed by CFK's successor, Mauricio Macri, made the problem abstract, as he conveniently adjusted the regulation to fit the needs of Grupo Clarín.

Mega-merger and Tailor-made Rules (2015–2020)

A look at the media map at the end of the second CFK administration in December 2015, the starting point for Macri (after winning in a tight election representing the *Cambiemos*Alliance, made up of PRO, UCR and Civic Coalition parties), shows some sort of shared patronage over the mutation of the media ecosystem in which some species disappeared and others emerged. Among those that survived, there have been considerable changes in their size, location, alignment and perspectives. This shared custody refers not only to the two governments with opposite ideologies (CFK and Macri) but also to the impact of digitization and platformization of communications around the world, as well as public policy management in Argentina. In other words, there has been not only "political" responsibility in the modifications of the sector but also policymaking in a context of radical transformations (Castells, 2009).

With Macri, Grupo Clarín landed in telecommunications with the merger between Cablevisión and Telecom (Becerra, 2018), after having tried the experiment of Nextel (a mobile communications firm with a small number of users, which Grupo Clarín bought at the end of the Kirchnerist era, a transaction that Macri approved in his second month in office), which was tepid compared to the new, gigantic and truly "convergent" concentration.

People curious about communication policies wondered in the brief period between the October 2015 elections and the inauguration of Macri in December of that year about the ability of the new government to change the regulatory framework that Kirchnerism had left behind. Specifically, they wondered about the fate of the Audiovisual Communication Services Law and the less discussed Argentine Digital Law (telecommunications and ICT) approved by Congress in 2014. One might think, given the PRO"s legislative minority, that the laws for the sector would not be quickly altered.

However, the leading group surrounding Macri made it clear from day one that communications constituted a strategic area and that they would in no way accept the legacy received. For the first time in Argentine history, a Ministry of Communications was created, which served as a beachhead to alter the administrative hierarchy of the sector. Led by Oscar Aguad, the ministry rooted out principles and regulations that prevented higher levels of concentration in the sector, paved the way for Grupo Clarín to carry out a new expansionary stage and was dissolved 18 months later. This implied that planning for the future and managing conflicts in the communications field were no longer a government priority. The job was done.

Despite the republican rhetoric of respect for the division of powers, the Macri administration conducted public policymaking in the field of communications through decrees and unilateral resolutions – some contradictory with each other – that disturbed the rules of the game. These became the precedents for the alteration of rules with each change of government, embodying the specter of the so-called "institutional instability" as never before (*Media Ownership Monitor*, 2019). In fact, Alberto Fernández, who defeated Macri in the elections at the end of 2019, has also signed decrees that shaped his own policy in the context of the Covid pandemic. Neither Grupo Clarín nor the employer associations it influences (the Association of Argentine Journalistic Entities, ADEPA; the Inter-American Press Association, SIP, or the Argentine Association of Cable Television, ATVC) have complained about the "institutional instability" caused by Macri with his decrees and resolutions. Instead, they protested against the laws voted on by Congress during the CFK administrations and against the 2020 decrees of Alberto Fernández, which reveals their double standards and implies that the alleged legal institutional instability was a pretext.

Macri created a new regulatory authority directly controlled by the National Executive Power, relaxed the regulations that limited concentration and extended the sector's licenses for five years (other presidents had taken that course before, for example, Kirchner through Necessity and Urgency Decree No. 527/2005). With surgical precision (since most of the articles of the Audiovisual Services Law continued in force) and without public debate, Macri substantially changed a law that had long been under the scrutiny of Argentine society. Following the shock caused by Necessity and Urgency Decree No. 267/15, the government promised to citizens and to the Inter-American Commission on Human Rights to send a bill to the National Congress that would give legislators their regulatory capacity back. That promise was never kept (*Media Ownership Monitor*, 2019).

Macri's communication policy took a 180-degree turn on the issues promoted by Kirchnerism. The discourse on the democratization of the media was abandoned and replaced by the rationale of market development and the need to attract investment. Over time, the promotion of convergence was included as a guiding principle for greater efficiency in the sector, which, according to the diagnosis of the Macri administration, was "lagging behind." However, the successive patches made to meet Grupo Clarín's needs of expansion in the telecom space – celebrated by the Group with the Cablevisión-Telecom merger and lamented by its competitors Telefónica and Claro, always with directions from Madrid and Mexico – were not successful in designing a truly "convergent" regulatory framework.

Grupo Clarín completed the purchase of Nextel (initiated at the end of the CFK administration), returning to the telephony sector[10] in very favorable conditions. In addition to authorizing the purchase, Macri granted Grupo Clarín an additional benefit by allowing it to use 2.5 Ghz spectrum licenses for mobile telephony with Nextel, via the reallocation of use (which was framed as a sort of "criollo refarming"). Originally, these licenses could not be used for mobile telephony and therefore their value was considerably lower.

In August 2016, preparing the groundwork for the merger, Grupo Clarín split into two companies with the same majority shareholders, but dividing the assets into two different corporate structures: Grupo Clarín SA concentrates newspapers, television channels and radios – AGEA (*Clarín, Olé, La Razón, La Voz del Interior* and *Los Andes* newspapers), Artear (*Canal 13* and cable stations), *Radio Mitre*, IESA (*TyC Sports*) and CMD (digital media)– and Cablevisión Holdings includes cable TV services, internet connectivity and mobile communications.

Macri adapted the regulations to the needs of *Clarín*'s shareholders. In light of the Macri decrees and the actions taken by the Ministry of Communications and the government entity ENaCom, the convergence configuration was so selective that only those holding 70 percent of the lucrative pay TV market were able to take full advantage of it (Becerra and Mastrini, 2017).

Without having fulfilled the promise of presenting a new bill, but accomplishing the task of adapting the regulatory framework to the needs of the largest of the market operators, Macri paved the way for the mega-merger of Cablevisión and Telecom, the largest merger in the history of communications in Latin America (Becerra, 2018).

The analysis of Macri's communication policy shows intense activity in the sector. Large companies that claimed that "the best media law is the one that does not exist" reveled in the rain of decrees. As politics are not neutral, Macri's policies had winners and losers. The main beneficiary once again was Grupo Clarín, which saw the limits to its expansion disappear, as access to new markets was facilitated, asymmetrical regulations for other large groups facilitated its take-off in telecommunications and some of its competitors reduced their positions (for instance, the sale of *Telefé* by Telefónica to Viacom in 2016). The merger between Grupo Clarín and Telecom, where the Group has operational control, was the icing on the cake.

With the merger, Grupo Clarín came to dominate at the national level with 42 percent of fixed telephony, 34 percent of mobile telephony, 56 percent of broadband internet connections, 35 percent of mobile connectivity and 40 percent of pay TV in 2018 (and this data had not changed substantially by the end of 2020). No other company had similar market power. Not to mention the fact that print, radio and television media further increased *Clarín*'s bargaining power due to their influence on public opinion.

Grupo Clarín was the great winner in the media market in the Macri era because of everything it bought and for what its competitors sold. In this way, the distance between the Group and its most immediate competitor has widened even more. And, above all, its media outlets have had an unparalleled position in shaping public opinion.

Once again, the editorial line of the media was put at the service of corporate expansion. War journalism, which permeated the work environment and the products themselves, caused considerable declines in the turnover of content production units, which were offset by the income from cable TV and internet connectivity.

Zoon Politikon

The Aristotelian concept of "political animal" to distinguish the human species from other animal species is very appropriate to depict the evolution of Clarín in its 75-year-long history. One of its great qualities throughout decades of enormous socio-cultural, political and economic changes was its resilience and adaptive capacity, evidenced in the founding and consolidation years of the newspaper led by Roberto Noble, as well as in the no less traumatic transition conducted after his death by the developmentalist thinkers led by Rogelio Frigerio, and in the subsequent – and current – expansive phase, from multimedia and to full convergence, led by Héctor Magnetto.

For Borrat, the sphere of action of every newspaper is naturally an act of influence: "A newspaper operationalizes its ability to affect the behavior of certain actors in a way that is favorable to its own interests: It influences the government, as well as political parties, stakeholders, social movements, the members of its audience" (1989: 67). *Clarín* may well be an exemplary case corroborating Borrat's thesis, as well as Noble''s alleged pronouncement after Frondizi's fall, namely, "I can no longer be president, I can make presidents."

Indeed, the relationships between Grupo Clarín and the various Argentine governments are key to understanding its development over the decades. Although in the beginning, the newspaper was politically linked to the so-called developmentalism (a movement that promoted industrialism and development of the domestic market), it had sufficient editorial breadth to be a group supporting the ruling party, especially at the beginning of the various presidential terms.

It was only openly confrontational during two periods: At the end of the Carlos Menem administrations and during the two terms served by CFK. While the first was a confrontation with an economic policy model that affected the Group's sales, the second one had to do with a more general political disagreement, which led Grupo Clarín to confront and seek revenge from the next administration, that of Mauricio Macri, who exponentially facilitated the expansion of the conglomerate.

Grupo Clarín's political history presents, through clearly discernible stages, common logical connectors. The link with the political establishment, the organic economic reliance on different governments to promote business growth in these stages, together with the generation of a massive market of readers later complemented with the construction of equally massive, broad, multi-class audiences identified with the national imaginary of development, characterized the evolution of Clarín until the final years of the 20th century.

Since the turn of the century, the progressive financierization of the communications ecosystem and the advent of technological convergence across media, telecommunications and the internet have been leveraged by the Group's leadership, driving its multimedia concentration and the reorganization of its revenue streams, and, consequently, of its corporate interests, thus giving its relations with the political establishment a wake-up call and shaping in a more defined way the editorial line of its already numerous media outlets.

Indeed, the last 20 years show much more aggressive positions against eventual government obstacles and against competitors perceived as threats to the expansive dynamics of the conglomerate led by Magnetto, at the expense of subordinating journalistic work to what the former editor-in-chief of the newspaper, Julio Blanck, called "war journalism," and reporting a loss of the relative influence of the Group's journalistic products in its overall income.

As this historical overview indicates, Grupo Clarín carries politics under its skin – ambivalent toward the first Perón era, friendly with the first Menem term and with Néstor Kirchner, militantly in favor of Frondizi and Macri, a good mate of the dictatorships of Aramburu and Onganía, a partner of the Videla dictatorship, distant from Alfonsín and Illia, an enemy of CFK and an adversary of the second Menem term.

Grupo Clarín's political performance has been both effective and responsive to the intense ups and downs of national politics, whose logic it has understood and supported, and has outdone not only other Argentine companies, most of which are small firms that have been competing with Grupo Clarín for at least 45 years, but also large international conglomerates, such as Telefónica or Claro. In the championship of the Argentine *zoon politikon*, Grupo Clarín is unrivaled.

Notes

1 The founding motto of the newspaper was "A wake-up call for the Argentine solution to Argentine problems."
2 Frondizi, from the Radical Party (UCR Party, stood out in the developmental branch of the party when it was divided into *Unión Cívica Radical del Pueblo* (UCRP) and *Unión Cívica Radical Intransigente* (UCRI), which would lead him to be a candidate in the elections organized by the dictatorship of Aramburu (self-proclaimed "Liberating Revolution") of 1958, in which he triumphed with the support of Peronism, which was banned. He governed the country between May 1, 1958 and March 29, 1962, when he was overthrown by a coup.
3 Later on, Camilion was an official of the dictatorship, first ambassador to Brazil, then chancellor, and, in the 1990s, Carlos Menem's defense minister, against whom Clarín published allegations of arms trafficking in 1995.
4 The origin of Papel Prensa dates back to the dictatorship of Juan Carlos Onganía through the provision of the Fund for the Development of Pulp and Paper Production (1969), financed with a 10 percent tax on paper imports. "All of the country's newspapers paid, for ten years, 10 percent of their imports to set up a plant that, finally, was only awarded to some of them," wrote Jorge Lanata (2008). Lanata pointed out, "In 1976, through front men, Graiver controlled all of Papel Prensa." His heirs were forced to transfer the shares to *La Nación, La Razón* and *Clarín*.

> The transfer to the three newspapers was signed on January 18, 1977. After transferring the shares, the members of the Graiver Group were arrested and all their assets were embargoed to prevent any claim by heirs from affecting the ownership of *Clarín* and its partners (…) The Graivers did not even collect the transfer of the shares. Thanks to the dictatorship, the newspapers obtained two loans: from Banco Español del Río de la Plata and Banco Holandes Unido, Geneva branch, for 7,200,000 dollars, just with a signature and without guarantees.
> (Lanata, 2008)

Between 1975 and 1976, the State also facilitated, with BANADE loans that were never repaid, the construction of Papel de Tucumán SA, which would allow the production of newsprint (an objective that was not achieved) for smaller media, such as the Kraiselburd group.
5 Ernestina Herrera was briefly detained in this case in 2002. Horacio Verbitsky wrote at the time, "The files investigated a quarter of a century later by Judge Marquevich due to allegations by *Abuelas de Plaza de Mayo* are a catalog of irregularities." The case was resolved when, after long resisting the DNA test of the then young Marcela and Felipe with the genetic data bank that has samples of some missing persons kidnapped by the dictatorship, both Noble Herrera heirs agreed to have their DNA tested only when it was confirmed – as Mochkovsky (2011) documents – that compatibility would not be demonstrated with that bank.

6 In November 2017, *Clarín* and *La Nación*, as main shareholders, resolved to close down DyN Agency.
7 Decree 22285/80 issued by Videla prevented print media companies from exploiting audiovisual licenses, a strategy to contain cross-concentration, designed to prevent Héctor Ricardo García, from *Crónica*, from recovering the license for *Canal 11* in Buenos Aires that he had acquired in 1970 and which was expropriated in 1975.
8 At the beginning of March 2008, the government announced a package of measures, including Resolution 125 of the Ministry of the Economy, which regulated the tax on mobile withholdings on soybean and sunflower exports. The announcement was made on March 11, just four months after CFK took office as President (she won 46 percent of the votes) and the period initiated with the aforementioned measure meant a break in the administration's plans away from the realignment of political, social and economic positions and alliances; a radically different scenario was configured, and it was the beginning of a political and social polarization that has continued to the present day.
9 Established in 2009 by the CFK administration, *Fútbol para Todos* was a program enabling access to the transmission of big league Argentine soccer tournaments and *Libertadores* Cup finals and semifinals, which was discontinued by Macri in 2017. The program was established through an agreement with the Argentine Soccer Association (owner of the soccer matches screening rights), which in 2009 ended its contract with Televisión Satelital Codificada (TSC) company – owned 50-50 by Grupo Clarín and Torneos y Competencias – precisely in the framework of the war between Kirchnerism and Grupo Clarín. It had a major impact as it enabled free access of the population to these sport shows. The *Fútbol para Todos* program was a precursor of the debates in the National Congress for the Audiovisual Communication Services Law.
10 Until the 2001 crisis, Grupo Clarín had been the owner of Compañía de Teléfonos del Interior (CTI), which was purchased by Mexican Carlos Slim to give birth to Claro.

References

Becerra, Martín (2015). *De la concentración a la convergencia. Políticas de medios en Argentina y América Latina*. Buenos Aires: Paidós.
Becerra, Martín (2018). "Trilogía sobre la megafusión Cablevisión-Telecom"; in *Letra P*.https://martinbecerra.wordpress.com/2018/05/30/trilogia-sobre-la-megafusion-cablevision-telecom/
Becerra, Martín and Guillermo Mastrini (2017). *La concentración infocomunicacional en América Latina (2000–2015). Nuevos medios y tecnologías, menos actores*. Bernal: UNQ -OBSERVACOM.
Borrat, Héctor (1989). "El periódico, actor del sistema político," *Análisis No. 12*, Universitat Autónoma de Barcelona, pp. 67–80.
Borrelli, Marcelo (2011).*El diario Clarín frente a la política económica de Martínez de Hoz (1976–1981)*, mimeo, Doctoral Thesis, School of Social Sciences, UBA.

Borrelli, Marcelo and Jorge Saborido (2013). "Por una dictadura desarrollista: el periódico Clarín frente a la política económica del último gobierno de facto en Argentina (1976–1981)," in *Studia Historica. Historia Contemporánea* n°31, Universidad de Salamanca, pp. 195–218. https://revistas.usal.es/index.php/0213-2087/article/view/14598/15052

Castells, Manuel (2009). *Comunicación y Poder*. Madrid: Alianza.

Lanata, Jorge (2008). "La historia se escribe en papel," in *Diario Crítica de la Argentina*, April 13, Buenos Aires.

Marino, Santiago (2013).*Políticas de comunicación del sector audiovisual: las paradojas de modelos divergentes con resultados congruentes*, mimeo, Doctoral Thesis, School of Social Sciences, UBA, March 2013.

Mastrini, Guillermo and Martín Becerra (eds.) (2017).*Medios en guerra: balance, crítica y desguace de las políticas de comunicación 2003–2016*.Buenos Aires: Biblos.

Media Ownership Monitor (2019). "La era Macri: la ley del mercado," en *Argentina*, Reporteros sin Fronteras and*Tiempo Argentino*.http://argentina.mom-rsf.org/es/hallazgos/legislacion-de-medios/

Mochkofsky, Graciela (2011). *Pecado original. Clarín, los Kirchner y la lucha por el poder*. Buenos Aires: Planeta.

Molinas, Ricardo and Fernando Molinas (1993). *Detrás del espejo: quince años de despojo al patrimonio nacional*.Buenos Aires: Beas.

Rincón, Omar (2010). "La obsesión porque nos amen: crisis del periodismo/éxitos de los telepresidentes", in Amado Suárez, Adriana (ed.). *La palabra empeñada: investigaciones sobre medios y comunicación pública en Argentina* (pp. 13–16). Buenos Aires: Friedrich Ebert Stiftung.

Sivak, Martín (2013). *Clarín. Una historia*. Buenos Aires: Planeta.

Sivak, Martín (2015). *Clarín. La era Magnetto*. Buenos Aires: Planeta.

Verbitsky, Horacio (2002), "El oro y el barro. La sórdida disputa por el caso Clarín," in *Página 12*, December 22.https://www.pagina12.com.ar/diario/elpais/1-14482-2002-12-22.html

3 Economic Profile

Corporate Structure

Grupo Clarín is the most significant cross-media conglomerate in Argentina. Its 75-year history began in 1945 with the creation of *Clarín* newspaper and its subsequent consolidation in the press sector, followed by an expansion into the broadcasting and telecommunications market segments.

In its first 30 years of existence, *Clarín* became the broadest circulation newspaper in Argentina. From the 1970s onward, it embarked on a process of expansion, in which five different stages can be identified. First, *Clarín* increased its activity in the press segment with the acquisition of a paper mill. Later, in the 1980s, it ventured into broadcasting (radio and free-to-air TV) and, during the 1990s and early 2000s, it expanded more aggressively into cable TV and internet services while also forging alliances with content production companies and making inroads into the telecommunications sphere. During the first decade of the 21st century, Grupo Clarín not only managed to solidify its position as a double-play services provider (cable TV and internet), but also began a process of technological overhauling and shifted its business model toward internet service provision. The launching of the newspaper portal clarin.com in the 1990s was the stepping stone to the digitization of Grupo Clarín's cable networks and media, continuing later with HD broadcasts of its TV channels (*Canal 13* and *Todo Noticias* (TN)). The year 2016 was a landmark year in the history of the Group because of some key events: The acquisition of Nextel and the merger of Cablevisión and Telecom. These events positioned Grupo Clarín in the lead in both mobile and landline communications and connectivity.

This process of expansion was achieved due to an aggressive strategy of risk-based growth (low-cost indebtedness) and reinvestment in the business, which was implemented by Héctor Magnetto, the main shareholder and the Group's CEO since 1999 (Mochkofsky, 2011). This strategic vision also found support in the public policies fostered by different government administrations, which created a favorable environment for said growth.

The expansion of the business and the search for resources to finance it was also a driving force behind the changes in Grupo Clarín's corporate structure. Although it retains the typical family-run business structure that characterizes Latin American groups, it is possible to highlight four crucial events concerning the capital composition of the Group.

In 1999, following the complex process of multimedia expansion, Grupo Clarín became a *sociedad anónima* [corporation], and caught the attention of investment bank Goldman Sachs, which became a shareholder. A few years later, in 2007, Grupo Clarín launched an Initial Public Offering (IPO), which was possible through the merger of the two largest cable TV providers in Argentina, Cablevisión and Multicanal, which had taken place in 2006 and had paved the way for the partnership with David Martínez, the Mexican-American investor who financed the operation by means of his fund Fintech Advisory. From that moment onward, Cablevisión was jointly owned by Grupo Clarín (60 percent of the stock) and Fintech (the remaining 40 percent). The third event took place nearly ten years later, in 2016, when Grupo Clarín announced the split-up of Cablevisión into a new corporation under the name of Cablevisión Holding (CVH), which would be in charge of the development of the infrastructure sector, and Grupo Clarín (GC), which would be responsible for content production. Finally, in 2017, the communications regulator *Ente Nacional de Comunicaciones* (ENACOM), created by former president Mauricio Macri, unanimously approved the merger between Cablevisión and Telecom, which obtained its final approval from the antitrust authority in June 2018 and cleared the way for the merger to occur. In both cases, there were statutory requirements for the merger by absorption, such as allowing third parties to use the new company's infrastructure to offer internet and other services, and the return of spectrum in wireless broadband and commercial conditions for the offer of bundled quadruple play services (cable TV, internet, landline and cell phone service), among others. In addition, the ruling of *Comisión Nacional de Defensa de la Competencia* (CNDC, Argentine Antitrust Commission), which reports to the Secretariat of Commerce, required the new company to divest its broadband business in 28 locations in the provinces of Córdoba, Buenos Aires, Entre Ríos, Misiones and Santa Fe.

56 *Economic Profile*

Since the merger, Grupo Clarín has included not only *Clarín* but also the spun-off Cablevisión Holding and Telecom. Hence, it has become Argentina's largest cross-media communications conglomerate, with a dominant position in the provision of cable TV, broadband connectivity, mobile communications, free-to-air TV space, radio and press services.

This chapter will analyze the economic profile of Grupo Clarín. Considering its expansion process, largely based on indebtedness and ongoing investment in the business, it is possible to state that the content production area has given way to the development of infrastructure, which has become central to the growth and expansion strategy of the Group.

To delve into this analysis, the history of Grupo Clarín will be broken down into four different periods or stages: 1945–1988, the monomedia stage of expansion; 1989–2006, the multimedia stage; 2007–2015, the bet on infrastructure and digitization; and, lastly, 2016–2020, full convergence. This last stage, which mainly revolved around the Cablevisión-Telecom merger, could in fact become the stepping stone that would grant Grupo Clarín the necessary funds to tackle its international expansion, as opposed to the strategy the Group has been following for the past 75 years, focusing solely on the national sphere.

Before plunging into the analysis, a thorough description of the corporate structure, the relevant lines of business and the Group's involvement in each one of them is offered below.

Capital Structure. Shareholders, Board of Directors and Management

The name Grupo Clarín refers to the group comprised of *Clarín* plus Cablevisión-Telecom: A national communications giant run by one group of controlling shareholders.

The Group's corporate structure builds upon preexistent familial and personal relationships between the main shareholders – a typical feature of Latin American groups – and a group of executives who are also members of the Board of Directors in the different corporations and hold managerial positions. Furthermore, the executive management of the Group is yet another clear expression of the relevance ascribed to infrastructure in its strategic vision. Nowadays, Magnetto's trusted collaborators, who have been together with him since the 1990s and have made significant contributions to the growth and expansion of the cable TV segment, hold the executive-level positions.

In 2016, the Group announced its split-up into two different organizations: Cablevisión Holding (CVH), which would be in charge of the development of infrastructure (cable TV, broadband and fixed

Economic Profile 57

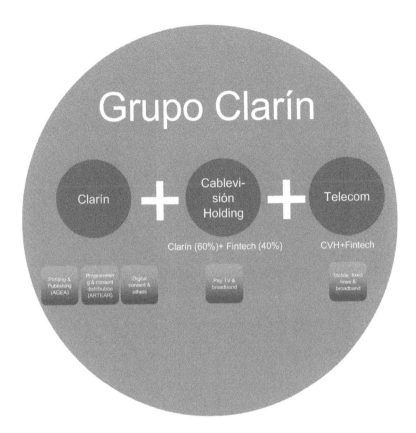

Figure 1 Grupo Clarín structure.

and mobile communication services), and Grupo Clarín (GC), which would be responsible for content (publishing, production and distribution of content). The split-up would be followed by the merger of Cablevisión Holding and Telecom Argentina in 2017.

In spite of this spin-off, both corporations have retained the same group of shareholders, namely, the historical controlling shareholders Marcela and Felipe Noble Herrera (heirs of the equity interest of Ernestina Herrera de Noble, widow of Noble), Magnetto, José Antonio Aranda and Lucio Rafael Pagliaro. Jointly, they own 71 percent of Clarín's shares (Magnetto holds a 29.8 percent equity interest and is thus the majority shareholder),[1] 9 percent is owned by the investment group Goldman Sachs, which acquired said stock by means of an agreement signed in 1999, and the remaining 20 percent of shares

58 *Economic Profile*

is free float. As regards CVH, the controlling shareholders own 77.5 percent of the stock whereas the remaining 22.5 percent of the shares is free float.

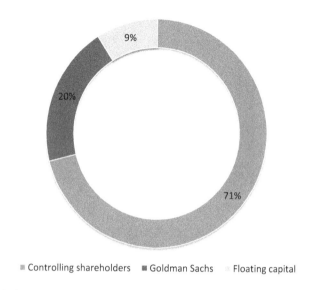

Figure 2 Grupo Clarín shareholders.

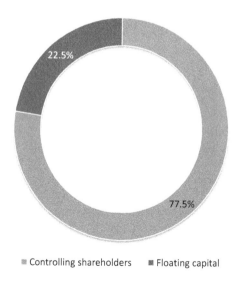

Figure 3 CVH shareholders.

Likewise, Figure 4 clearly illustrates the shareholder structure of Telecom Argentina: Fintech Advisory (hedge fund owned by Martínez) holds 20.38 percent of the shares; CVH owns 28.16 percent of the shares; a trust set up by Magnetto and Martínez holds 21.84 percent and the remaining 29.15 percent are publicly traded shares.

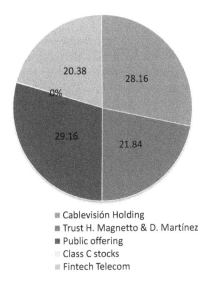

- Cablevisión Holding
- Trust H. Magnetto & D. Martínez
- Public offering
- Class C stocks
- Fintech Telecom

Figure 4 Telecom Argentina shareholders.

The presence and influence of the shareholders is also notable in the boards of the different corporations, which were responsible for the design of the policies and general strategies of the Group. These boards are composed by the shareholders themselves, as well as their family members and other individuals who have held management positions in Grupo Clarín, particularly since the 1990s. This is clearly evidenced in the regular members of the Board,[2] who hold the "Class A Shares" (those shares with more voting rights and dividend priority).

According to the minutes of the last Annual General Meeting of Shareholders which was available in late 2020, CVH's Board of Directors is composed of the following members: Sebastián Bardengo[3] (Chair), Ignacio Sáenz Valiente[4] (Vice Chair), Marcela Noble Herrera,

Marcia Magnetto, Lucio Pagliaro and Antonio Aranda (descendants of the main shareholders). All of them own "Class A" Shares (Cablevisión, April 30, 2020).

By the same token, the Class A Shares of Grupo Clarín are owned by the following members of its Board: Jorge Rendo[5] (Chair), Héctor Aranda[6] (Vice Chair), Felipe Noble Herrera, Horacio Magnetto, Francisco Pagliaro and Alma Aranda (descendants of the main shareholders) (Clarín, May 4, 2020).

The composition of Telecom's board is a clear reflection of the interests of its main shareholders, Clarín and Fintech. The Executive Directors are, predominantly, persons who have been historically linked to Clarín (particularly through Cablevisión) and, to a lesser degree, individuals who are close to the main shareholder, Martínez (Fintech). Its members are Carlos Moltini (Chair), a key player in Cablevisión's expansion; Mariano Ibáñez[7] (Vice Chair), Martínez' close collaborator; Alejandro Urricelqui[8] (who formerly worked at Cablevisión); Sebastián Bardengo (who also chairs CVH's Board, as previously stated); Damián Cassino[9] (Clarín); Carlos Harrison[10] (Clarín); Martín D'Ambrosio[11]; Germán Vidal[12]; Luca Luciani[13]; Baruki Luis González[14]; and Eduardo de Pedro. The latter is the current Minister of Internal Affairs of Argentina, who acts as the state's representative before the Board representing the minority stock owned by the state through *Administración Nacional de Seguridad Social* (ANSES, the National Social Security Administration).

The similarities between Clarín and Cablevisión-Telecom are found not only in their equity and Board composition, but also at the management level. After the split-up of Grupo Clarín and CVH, several senior executives from Clarín (Cablevisión) began holding key management positions in Telecom. Some examples are included here by way of illustration.

At the beginning of Macri's administration, Martínez was granted the authorization to purchase shares in Telecom. Martínez' ownership of stock brought along a renewal in the upper echelons of the firm's management, which now included members such as Roberto Nobile, former Chief Operations Officer at Cablevisión, who took on the position of Strategy, Innovation and Business Development Officer of Telecom (Telecom, May 12, 2016; Bizberge, 2017). Recently, Nobile has replaced Moltini as CEO of Telecom. Moltini had been CEO of Cablevisión before becoming CEO and Chairman of the Board of Telecom (*Cronista*, January 7, 2020; *Infobae*, May 21, 2020).

Economic Profile 61

When the merger between Cablevisión and Telecom was approved in 2017, there was a significant increase in the number of executives who held positions in the management of the new corporation and who had been historically linked to Grupo Clarín: Apart from Moltini's appointment as CEO of Telecom (who was subsequently replaced by Nobile in January 2020), and, more recently as Chair of the firm's Board; Gonzalo Hita, former Sales Manager of Fibertel, became the Chief Operations Officer of Telecom; Juan Martín Vico, former Chief Financial Officer of Cablevisión, was appointed to the same position at Telecom; whereas Hernán Verdaguer became Telecom's Director of Regulatory Affairs.

Figure 5 shows a summary of the management structure of both Clarín and Telecom.

Based on all the information analyzed in this section, there is enough evidence to support the statement that Grupo Clarín has

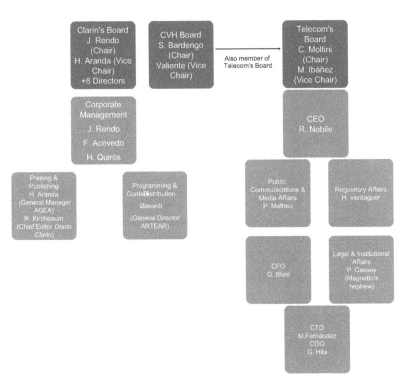

Figure 5 Clarín & Telecom management structure.

maintained the characteristics of a family-run business group that is typical of Latin American media conglomerates, albeit with certain nuances. Unlike other regional groups, such as Globo in Brazil, Televisa in Mexico or Cisneros in Venezuela, which exhibit a patriarchal line of succession (Sinclair, 1999), it was Ernestina Herrera, Noble's widow, who took the helm at an early stage of Clarín, and was later followed by her children Marcela and Felipe. Nevertheless, the stewardship of the business, at both the executive and shareholding levels, has been in the hands of Magnetto, who is unrelated to the family lineage and does not come from a well-to-do family (neither did Noble, the Group's founder). Magnetto has led the transformation of the firm into a multimedia group with diversified interests within the telecom sector.

Likewise, the relevance of a family business logic becomes evident when taking a closer look at the membership of the boards of the different corporations in the Group, given the fact that the successors of Magnetto, Noble, Aranda and Pagliaro are either kin or other highly trusted group members. Notably, in the case of Telecom, it is possible to distinguish clearly how the positions of power are divided between executives who are close to Martínez and executives who are close to Magnetto.

One rung down the ladder, executive management positions are also held by individuals who succeeded in forging strong, professional bonds in the Group. This was particularly the case after the Cablevisión-Telecom merger, when executives who were historically linked to the growth of the cable TV corporation landed key positions in the business.

The next section provides a detailed account of the dominant position held by Grupo Clarín in the different lines of business it offered in the Argentine market following the merger of Clarín, Cablevisión and Telecom.

Lines of Business and Market Share

Grupo Clarín is a benchmark service provider in the industry with a footprint that spans across media market segments (broadcast and pay TV, radio, newspapers and magazines) as well as telecommunications market segments (broadband connectivity and fixed and mobile communications). In spite of having competitors across them all, it is the strongest player in most segments and the only one with such breadth and depth of service and delivery (Becerra and Mastrini, 2017: 81).

Economic Profile 63

The picture of the current structure of the market of info-communication services in Argentina clearly shows that Grupo Clarín is not only the leading provider of broadband internet and cable TV services, but it also owns leading broadcast TV channels, radio stations and newspapers and magazines.

According to the statistics published by the regulator for the first quarter of 2020, there are 8.81 million broadband internet connections in the country today, distributed among service providers Cablevisión-Telecom (46 percent market share), the undisputed leader of the segment; Telefónica (15 percent); Telecentro (12 percent) and Supercanal (7 percent). Cablevisión managed to consolidate its supremacy due to the favorable regulatory reforms introduced by Macri's administration as well as the Cablevisión-Telecom merger, which enabled the firm to increase its lead in the market (Bizberge, September 1, 2020).

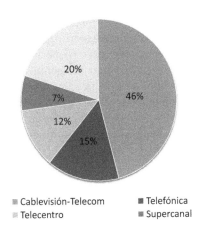

Figure 6 Market share – fixed broadband.

As regards cable TV, Cablevisión is still the largest network in the market in terms of subscriptions with a total 9.7 million subscribers in the first quarter of 2020, although in past years it has been losing its competitive edge (while still expanding in absolute terms) due to the increasing popularity of DirecTV and competition from online VOD service providers. Currently, Cablevisión holds a 38 percent market share, followed closely by DirecTV (31 percent), whose penetration rate in Argentina increased in 2013, fueled mainly by its growth with its pre-paid TV service, and continued to accelerate in 2014 and 2015 after being acquired by AT&T (Bizberge, September 1, 2020).

64 *Economic Profile*

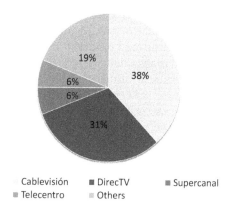

Figure 7 Market share – pay TV.

In mobile communications, there are 56 million mobile cellular lines in the country, which means a user penetration rate of nearly 124 percent. Today, the main players are Claro (América Móvil), which holds a 39 percent market share, Personal (Telecom-Cablevisión), 31 percent, and Movistar (Telefónica), 29 percent. Claro's leading position in the market can be explained by its growth in the pre-paid segment – the user-preferred service in Argentina – due to its improvements in network coverage after winning spectrum auctions and placing new antennas (Bizberge, September 1, 2020).

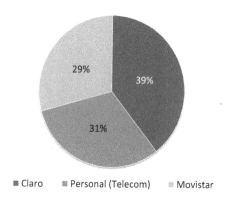

Figure 8 Market share – mobile lines.

In the press and radio market segments, the national audience concentration level of the top four players is 46.25 percent (considering traditional media outlets, radio and television): Grupo Clarín is at the forefront, controlling 25.28 percent of the total aggregate audience across all media, followed by América and Viacom (approximately 7 percent each), and Indalo (6.6 percent of the market) (*Tiempo Argentino* and RSF, 2019).

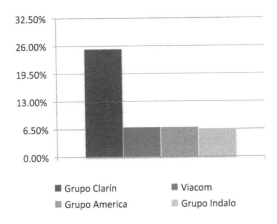

Figure 9 Aggregate audiences for press and broadcasting.

In the newspaper and magazine market segment, *Clarín* has been the newspaper with the largest circulation for the past 40 years. Although its market share has reduced to about 20 percent, it is still the dominant group in print media and it holds top position in the online media segments (*Tiempo Argentino* and RSF, 2019). Together, *Clarín* newspaper, *La Voz del Interior* in the province of Córdoba and *Los Andes* in the province of Mendoza (all of them Grupo Clarín media outlets) held 47.8 percent of audiences and 40 percent of state advertising in 2018 (*Tiempo Argentino* and RSF, 2019). As regards the distribution of official advertising investment, the administrations of Mauricio Macri (2015–2019) and Alberto Fernández (currently in office) have both granted Grupo Clarín the largest share (Espada and Marino, October 11, 2020).

As for free-to-air TV space, *Canal 13*, which belongs to Grupo Clarín, is the second most watched television channel, whereas the forerunner is Telefé (acquired by Viacom in 2016). However, when considering the Group's media outlets in open and pay TV jointly,[15] they hold the highest levels of audience concentration (22.6 percent), followed by the media outlets owned by Viacom[16] (15.1 percent) and América[17] (8.7 percent) (*Tiempo Argentino* and RSF, 2019).

66 *Economic Profile*

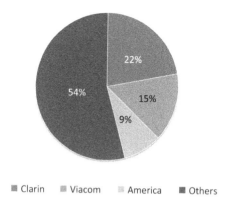

Figure 10 Market share – programming channels.

Although the radio market is more diversified than the TV market when it comes to media ownership, it is more concentrated in terms of audience. Grupo Clarín, through *Radio Mitre*, accounts for 41 percent of the audience concentration of AM radio stations, whereas *Radio La 100* is second behind *Pop 101.3* (Grupo Indalo) in the segment of FM stations (Becerra and Mastrini, 2017). Again, if AM and FM radio stations are considered jointly, the stations owned by Grupo Clarín hold 19.5 percent of audiences, followed by Grupo Indalo (14.6 percent), Prisa (12.4 percent), Grupo América (6.5 percent) and Cadena 3 (6.16 percent) (*Tiempo Argentino* and RSF, 2019).

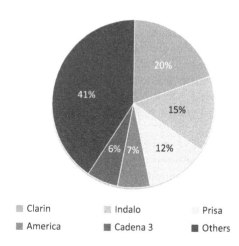

Figure 11 Market share – aggregate audiences AM-FM radio stations.

Last, but not the least, *Clarín* owns four out of six of the main digital media outlets in the country: The online portals of newspapers *Clarín* and *La Voz*, the website of the news channel TN and the most popular radio station – *La 100* (*Tiempo Argentino* and RSF, 2019).

Stages of the Integration Process

Grupo Clarín achieved the aforementioned level of consolidation by means of an expansion strategy that, from an analytical perspective, can be broken down into four different periods. Whereas it is true that this consolidation process found support in the public policies of different administrations that favored its growth, these periods have been defined following a business logic and hence they do not always match political periods:

- From its creation in 1945 to 1988. This is the monomedia stage, which focused mainly on the growth of the newspaper. The milestone of this stage was the establishment of a partnership with newspapers *La Razón* and *La Nación*, as well as the Argentine state, in the 1970s, to acquire the main paper mill for the country's newspapers, called Papel Prensa. This was followed by the creation of a news agency (called Diarios y Noticias, DyN, created jointly with *La Nación* and other newspapers) and entrance into the radio industry.
- From 1989 to 2006. This was the multimedia expansion stage, as Grupo Clarín entered and solidified its position in the content production, broadcast TV, radio and pay TV segments, and even ventured into broadband service provision segments of the market.
- From 2007 to 2015. The Group became a listed company on the stock exchange with the merger between Cablevisión and Multicanal, the country's main cable TV service providers, placing a very strong bet on infrastructure and digital convergence.
- From 2016 to the present. Over the past five years, a number of business decisions were made, the most relevant ones being the spin-off of the corporation ("split up to grow up") and the Cablevisión-Telecom merger, as well as the subsequent integration of the firms and their corporate cultures, in pursuit of full convergence.

Monomedia Expansion (1945–1988)

The first edition of *Clarín* newspaper came out on August 24, 1945. It cost the equivalent of USD 0.012[18] and it sold 160,000 copies. In spite of making a bright start, it still lagged far behind the circulation of the leading newspapers of the time, namely, *La Prensa* (370,000 copies), *El Mundo* (300,000) and *La Nación* (220,000) (Sivak, 2013: 50).

Although the newspaper's growth came with an increase in classified ads, its first 30 years were marked by a precarious financial position, which forced it to depend on state loans as well as on the price fluctuations of newsprint in the international market. *Clarín*'s luck would turn after the rather controversial purchase of Papel Prensa, which was negotiated by Magnetto, who acquired a stake in the corporation. This move was the triggering event behind *Clarín*'s expansion, which became more aggressive and solidified the Group's position during the 1990s.

During Perón's first term in office, the newspaper experienced significant growth, which continued during the self-proclaimed *Revolución Libertadora* ["Liberating Revolution," the coup d'état], with sales increasing by 20 percent between 1955 and 1956. Later, during the Frondizi administration (1958–1962), alignment with the president's ideals brought about significant financial benefits for the newspaper and it made an even greater leap: Its workforce increased from 46 employees in 1945 to 1,014 employees in 1960, and the number of copies sold rocketed from 304,000 to 370,000 between 1958 and 1961. This process of expansion slowed down with the fall of Frondizi (Sivak, 2013).

After Noble's death in 1969, the newspaper was hit by a severe economic crisis in 1971–1972. At that time, Magnetto, together with José Aranda and Lucio Pagliaro, took over the newspaper's management and tried to set its accounts straight.

In March 1971, driven by President Alejandro Lanusse, the Executive Branch called for tenders to build a pulp mill and, even though none of the bids met the capacity requirements, it ended up accepting an untimely offer made by the firm Papel Prensa SACIFyM, which belonged to César Civita (also the owner of publishing house Editorial Abril) (Sivak, 2013: 222). A victim of political pressures, Civita sold his shares in 1973 to Grupo Graiver – which was linked to different political factions, including the Peronist political-armed organization, *Montoneros*. Up to that time, *Clarín* had been shunned from Papel Prensa by Grupo Graiver – headed by David Graiver, who died in a rather mysterious airplane crash in Mexico, in 1976 – and José Ber Gelbard, Minister of Economy during Perón's third term, who controlled the firm (Sivak, 2013: 281).

Following Graiver's death, and as a result of pressure exerted by the military government, the shares of Papel Prensa were transferred to the state, which had partnered with newspapers *Clarín*, *La Nación* and *La Razón*. Today, Papel Prensa's equity is held by Clarín (49 percent of the shares, as it became the owner of *La Razón*'s stocks after its bankruptcy in the late 1980s), *La Nación* (22.5 percent) and the National state (27.5 percent plus 0.62 percent of equity owned by the state-run news agency *Telam*).

The military junta financed these newspapers so that they would keep the newsprint factory running by extending them loans from the National Development Bank, and by subsidizing the power consumption of the paper mill as well as by increasing the import tariffs on their raw material by 48 percent (Postolski and Marini, 2005: 173). The acquisition of Papel Prensa – which began operating in 1978 – became the solution to *Clarín*'s historical problem: The uncertainty associated with the availability of printing paper and its subjection to the fluctuation of international prices. Now, it had access to its basic raw material, newsprint, and it could control its price at will.

During the last dictatorship (1976–1983), *Clarín* became the broadest circulation newspaper and the leader in the classified ads business (Borrelli and Saborido, 2013). The average annual sales peaked and increased from 312,000 copies in 1976 to 392,000 in 1977, from 461,000 copies in 1978 to 497,000 in 1979, from 543,000 in 1981 to 611,000 in 1982 (Sivak, 2013: 314).

Because of the key role he played in the purchase of Papel Prensa, Magnetto gained the trust of Noble's widow, who rewarded him with equity in the corporation. From that moment onward, Magnetto was intent on transforming the newspaper into a multimedia group. That would eventually enable the Group to expand its scope of influence and profits by means of a risk-taking and reinvestment strategy, a rather unusual strategy for Argentine corporations (Mochkofsy, 2011).

In 1982, the Group created the news agency DyN. As the democratic elections drew near, heralding the end of the military coup, Magnetto had already planned for the next stage of the diversification, namely, the expansion into the broadcasting segment (the radio industry first and then the free-to-air TV space). However, pursuant to Broadcasting Law No. 22285, passed in 1980, which regulated audiovisual communication services, print media companies were forbidden from purchasing radio licenses; this was undoubtedly a setback to Magnetto's plans. Hence, he mounted a powerful lobby seeking to change the law – before and after the 1983 elections in which Raúl Alfonsín ascended to presidency – albeit with no success.

Economic Profile

1985 was the year in which *Clarín* enjoyed Latin America's largest readership and entered a new stage in its expansion by means of the acquisition of *Radio Mitre*, thus gaining access to the broadcasting market. This illicit operation, carried out by means of shell companies, became legitimate after partial changes were made to the Broadcasting Law during Carlos Menem's first term of office.

In the monomedia stage of expansion (1945–1988), *Clarín* consolidated its position in the press segment, as evidenced by the evolution of its distribution and sales (Table 1) and its process of vertical expansion, starting with the acquisition of Papel Prensa and its diversification into the broadcast market. Figure 12 summarizes the Group's expansion process during this period.

Table 1 Newspaper sales

	Newspaper sales
1945	160,000
1958	304,000
1961	370,000
1977	392,000
1978	461,000
1979	497,000
1980	543,000
1981	575,000
1982	611,000
1987	680,000

Source: Sivak (2013).

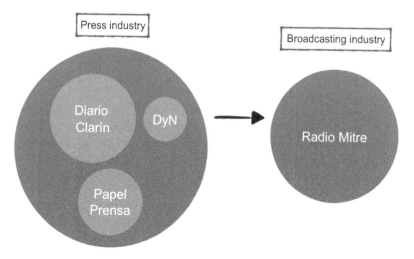

Figure 12 Clarín's first phase of expansion (1945–1988).

As it purchased Papel Prensa, the newspaper gained some autonomy from the initial political project albeit not from politics. Magnetto began to deploy a business-driven strategy but his expansive project required support from the state in order to thrive, as will be seen in the next stages of the diversification process.

Multimedia Expansion (1989–2006)

The expansion and consolidation of *Clarín* were favored by the media policies of the 1990s, during Menem's first and second consecutive terms in power (1989–1994 and 1995–1999), which strongly encouraged the concentration of capital and property ownership in only a few hands, first with the participation of domestic and, later on, foreign capital. As a result, toward the end of the decade, Grupo Clarín, together with Telefónica, strengthened their positions as the leading media groups in the country (Albornoz, 2000 and Mastrini and Becerra, 2006).

The newspaper, which already held equity in Papel Prensa and owned a radio station (*Mitre*), therefore expanded into the segments of free-to-air and pay TV (distribution system and signals, including the broadcast of soccer games) and internet service provision, and even made a fleeting foray into the cell phone market with its brief participation in the share capital of Compañía de Teléfonos del Interior (CTI).

This growth would not have been possible without reforms and changes in the regulatory environment. Law No. 23696 [the State Reform Law], enacted in 1989, paved the way for the privatization of free-to-air TV channels, which had until then been in the hands of the state. The provisions of this law introduced changes to some of the key aspects of the Broadcasting Law (Law No. 22,285) – in force until 2009 – and authorized the setup of media conglomerates by allowing media groups to provide audiovisual services. Thus, Grupo Clarín entered into the free-to-air TV space through Canal 13 and legitimized its ownership of *Radio Mitre*.

As Sivak explains, the shareholding composition of ARTEAR – the corporation which was awarded the license of *Canal 13*, whose controlling shareholder was Grupo Clarín – was a clear reflection of Magnetto's leadership, who at the time held a 25 percent equity interest, while Noble's widow held a 32 percent interest. The rest of the stock was held by AGEA (22 percent) and Invarar (40 percent), whose shareholding composition, in turn, included Herrera de Noble (15 percent of stock), Magnetto (31 percent), Aranda and Pagliaro (23 percent each), as well as other minority shareholders (Sivak, 2015: 141).

Likewise, in 1992 Grupo Clarín expanded to cable TV with the purchase of Multicanal, which had initially devised an expansion strategy based upon the acquisition of local cable television operators, thus laying the foundations for its subsequent indebtedness. This enabled Grupo Clarín to quickly position itself at the level of Cablevisión,[19] the leading player of the segment and its main competitor, with whom it would later join to purchase the third cable operator in the market, Video Cable Comunicación (VCC). In 1997, VCC was sold to Grupo Clarín (Multicanal) and Cablevisión, which at the time was owned by CEI-Telefónica, together with free-to-air TV channels 9 and 11, among others (Albornoz and Hernández, 2005). The growth of CEI-Telefónica had been strongly backed up by Menem; as Clarín had refused to support his campaign for a third consecutive term in office – he was finally barred constitutionally from doing so – Menem sought to give more power to an alternative group that could compete against the company founded by Noble (Mochkofsky, 2011: 128).

Besides penetrating the cable TV market, Grupo Clarín also became a player in the satellite TV segment as it paired with Grupo Liberty to acquire ownership in satellite television operator DirecTV (Group Clarín owned 51 percent of the shares). In 1994, it entered the mobile communications market as it acquired 25 percent of the stocks of CTI, the first provider of mobile communication services outside the metropolitan area, which was purchased in 2002 by América Móvil, the telephone company of Mexican business magnate Carlos Slim.

Clarín's alliance with Telefónica (through Multicanal) in the cable segment, together with its participation in CTI, is clear evidence of the Group's intention to enter the communications market, even if at this stage it was forced to sell its equity (DirecTV included) to settle its financial accounts and tackle the debts it had incurred to finance its expansion.

In the meantime, Grupo Clarín also ventured into the content creation market by partnering with content production companies and TV and film production companies: It created the news channel *Todo Noticias* (TN) in 1993 and *Canal Volver* in 1994; it entered the feature films segment through a partnership with ARTEAR and Pol-ka and acquired a stake in Patagonik in partnership with Buena Vista (Disney) in 2000 and it started a partnership with Ideas del Sur, yet another production company, in 2005.

In addition, the media conglomerate had also incorporated the internet service provider PRIMA (Ciudad Internet and Datamarkets) as well as CIMECO (a partnership between *Clarín* and *La Nación* to acquire the provincial newspapers *La Voz del Interior* and *Los Andes de Mendoza*), in addition to its participation in Papel Prensa, AGEA and ARTEAR.

By the end of the 1990s, the newspaper and cable services had become the Group's main sources of revenue, whereas free-to-air TV enabled it to have a strong impact on audiences (Mastrini, 2013).

Multicanal's growth gave Grupo Clarín the opportunity to achieve an economy of scale; on the one hand, this helped to lower its programming and equipment costs, and, on the other hand, it boosted its subscriptions, which, in turn, enabled it to obtain financing in the international stock market by issuing corporate bonds (Albornoz, 2000). The Group also requested loans from foreign banks, given the low interest rates charged at the time and the exchange rate stability in Argentina.

From 1998, within the context of recession, Grupo Clarín started to experience some financial setbacks, which were heightened with the depreciation of the Argentine peso against the US dollar and the devaluation of the national currency in 2002. Hence, Grupo Clarín was faced with a drop in the number of subscribers, triggered by the population's loss of purchasing power in the context of an economic crisis, as well as the dollarization of its costs and the pesification [conversion into Argentine pesos] of its revenue (Marino, 2017: 122).

Beset by the economic downturn of the country and burdened with its expansion mechanism (based on low-cost external indebtedness), the situation for Grupo Clarín was critical: The firm's annual billing was USD 2 billion and its reported debt was around USD 1.7 billion, which the Group managed to reduce to USD 1.2 billion after pulling back from CTI and DirecTV (Sivak, 2015: 314).

The Group's transformation into a *sociedad anónima* (corporation) and the admission of Goldman Sachs as a shareholder, both in 1999, were strategies deployed to reduce its debt and to find additional funding to continue its expansion in the cable TV market, which would become even more aggressive in 2006 with the purchase of a stake (60 percent) in Cablevisión (owned by the HTM&F fund at the time).

Before Argentina's default in 2002, Multicanal's debt amounted to USD 815 million, which was brought down to USD 680 million in July 2001, thanks to the injection of USD 150 million from its shareholders, after a dispute with creditors had been settled (Multicanal had defaulted on payments due). Likewise, AGEA's debt amounted to USD 408 million (Sivak, 2015: 339 and 405).

Following the social, political and economic crisis of 2001–2002, the Néstor Kirchner administration (2003–2007) tried to forge a positive relationship with the main media outlets in the country, particularly with Grupo Clarín. Those intentions were expressed through a series of regulations,[20] which enabled the Group to settle its debt and to seek new injections of capital to further finance its journey of expansion into full convergence.

Since the beginning of the 1990s, Grupo Clarín had placed a very high bet on the convergence of video, data and voice services, and it had taken three major steps to achieve it: The aforementioned alliance with Telefónica in the cable market segment, a failed partnership with Telecom and the Multicanal-Cablevisión merger. Martín Etchevers, Grupo Clarín's External Communications Manager, explained in an interview:

> We had to find a way to secure the market position Grupo Clarín had achieved through the acquisition of Multicanal in the 1990s… The diversity of operations we had acquired, together with the ones we had created, showed us that we had to make a bold, networked investment to be able to set foot on the so-called road to convergence… Even as the Group entered into its first strategic partnership with CEI-Telefónica,[21] we were fully convinced that we needed cash flow to develop the cable TV segment; Internet was still in its initial stage at the time. After CEI's spin-off, we knew that we would need support in the telecommunications market. First, we had some talks with Telecom Italy in 1998 to evaluate the possibility of a strategic partnership in Multicanal, but it did not follow through. Then we made a second attempt at entering the telecom networks space when Telefónica and CEI split up. We sought to partner up again with Telefónica in 2000, but it did not work out, either… We had a huge challenge, to consolidate our business either with a phone company or with a cable TV operator. We knew that Multicanal, because it had neither fixed nor mobile telecommunications and lacked the capital density needed to reach an investment power equal to that of telephone companies, was going to be a challenge. After the Cablevisión-Multicanal merger, we knew that we had a shot at becoming a fourth player in the telecoms market, dominated by Telefónica, Telecom and Claro, but to

do so we would have to introduce major improvements to our network... When the merger was approved, the management made a firm decision to place a high bet on improving networks, digitizing signals, incorporating HD signals and increasing the broadband spectrum efficiency of the Cablevisión-Multicanal network.[22]

In September 2006, the Cablevisión-Multicanal merger was finally accomplished, and the Secretariat of Commerce issued the final approval in December 2007. Thus, Grupo Clarín purchased the shares owned by the investment fund HTM&F in Cablevisión, equivalent to a 60 percent equity interest, and the remaining 40 percent was acquired by Fintech Advisory (Martínez). Likewise, Cablevisión held a 98.5 percent stake in Multicanal and was the sole proprietor of Teledigital, a cable TV operator in the provinces, and of Fibertel, the internet service provider. Furthermore, through Multicanal, the Group also became the owner of 97 percent of the shares of PRIMA, another internet service provider like Fibertel. Hence, Grupo Clarín now held more than 50 percent of the market share of cable TV, and one-third of the market share of broadband services, at the national level. This was a milestone in the Group's history and reflected the corporate decision to make a strong bet on infrastructure to achieve technological convergence.

As evidenced in Figure 13, which shows the results of Grupo Clarín's second phase of expansion (1989–2006), the Group was already a player in all the telecommunications market segments, with the exception of the mobile and landline phone segments, in which it was not able to stay for lack of capital.

This stage was characterized by a model of management based on the development of economies of scale and economies of scope by means of the acquisition and purchase of corporations and/or the establishment of partnerships with operators at a national and global scale.

To do so, Grupo Clarín deployed a strategy of expansion that focused on low-cost indebtedness through access to the international stock market. Also, the Group sought to exert influence in the political sphere and swing the balance in its favor by lobbying for the implementation of regulations that would contribute to its growth.

Clarín realized at an early stage that the bet on infrastructure was an essential precondition to keep on evolving in the telecommunications

Figure 13 Clarín's second phase of expansion (1989–2006).

business, which, in the 1990s, seemed to be pointing at convergence as its next destination.

Despite the adverse economic context of the country, which meant several limitations for the Group's indebtedness strategy, sometimes even threatening the Group's very existence, the CEO would argue that it was the only available option considering the lack of credit in Argentina (López, 2008; Sivak, 2015: 433).

The process of multimedia expansion that shaped this stage focused mainly on cable and internet networks, which required a considerable investment, because the leaders of the Group understood that it would be the springboard to new businesses in the face of digitization. At the same time, the Group's presence in the content market segment (first through the newspaper, and later through radio stations and TV channels) secured a powerful position from which to exert political influence in order to obtain benefits that would help it consolidate over time.

Clarín's Journey to Convergence (2007–2015)

The Cablevisión-Multicanal merger was key in the business strategy of Grupo Clarín in at least three ways: To increase the offer of cross-media services, to develop digital content and to expand the Group regionally, which is one of the objectives that was initially established when the company was listed in the Buenos Aires and London stock exchanges in October 2007.

The importance given by the Group to the development of infrastructure became evident because cable TV and internet have been its main sources of revenue since 2007. With the merger, Grupo Clarín had also bet on the convergence of services to include telephony – fixed telephony, at that time – in its service package. Nevertheless, there were limitations due to government policies that restricted access to frame numbering (a conflict that escalated during the dispute over the Audiovisual Communication Services Law of 2009), and also due to the telephone companies involved (Telefónica and Telecom), which blocked interconnection with their networks. Moreover, the Group's business strategy evolved and changed because, over time, fixed-line telephony became unattractive for company profitability, so it made little sense to invest in the necessary technology, which had become outdated as years went by (Bizberge, 2019: 355).

After the merger, and as part of the cross-media initiative, the Group created a specific unit to leverage digital businesses: Compañía de Medios Digitales (CMD). However, this line remained in a marginal position over the years, since it only represented roughly 3 percent of the Group's total revenue (Bizberge, 2015 and 2017). In fact, projects launched for the internet are not concentrated in CMD; instead, each unit has its know-how and full control in the development of its digitization process and the creation of its own content (Bizberge, 2015). As Etchevers explained:

> The Group's big investment in digital content was made at brand level (both in human resources and infrastructure); for example, ARTEAR's multiplatform studio, *Clarín* subscriptions and Big Data Department, the development of Cimeco's *Vía País*, etc. Early on, CMD was an industry of digital innovation and undertakings, but this was later transferred to each company for agility purposes. Except for the first period, when clarin.com was part of CMD, every business unit went on to manage their own digital sector. Our idea was to diversify the brands online, as we believed that was the best way to reach different audiences, and we did that

from the business units. The investment in TN [news channel] was made by ARTEAR; the investment in *Clarín*, by AGEA; and the *Cienradios* portal project [online radio menu which collects the Group's radio stations], by *Radio Mitre*.[23]

After the Cablevisión-Multicanal merger, Grupo Clarín went public in a quest for funds to tackle its regional expansion, which began in the late 1990s when the country's severe economic crisis had ended. Following the admission of Goldman Sachs in 1999, and when the negotiation for the payment to external bondholders (which had been a critical issue in the previous expansion stage, mainly with cable) was over, going public represented a milestone in the search for low-cost financing. When the Group had reached a solid presence in the national market, the project was to launch digital and cross-media services, and to expand beyond Argentine borders.

> When it went public, Grupo Clarín took a crucial step in its consolidation, regional expansion and growth strategy. Grupo Clarín's decision of listing part of its shares was aimed at financing future investments within its leadership strategy in the Argentine and Latin American media markets.
>
> (Grupo Clarín, 2007: 11)

However, unlike other large conglomerates of the region (such as Televisa, from México, or Grupo Globo, from Brazil), most of *Clarín*'s business is conducted in Argentina, and regional expansion has been limited to relatively small neighboring countries, Uruguay and Paraguay. In Uruguay, *Clarín* offers a subscription TV service and it is the main provider in Montevideo, the capital city. In Paraguay, the Group provided a pay TV service until 2012, when it sold the company to Millicom. Furthermore, following the merger between Cablevisión and Telecom in 2017, it offers cell phone services with the brand Núcleo, which was inherited from Telecom's operations.

One of the reasons why the Group's expansion in the regional market was hindered is that it was difficult to get the necessary funds due to the size of the Argentine market. On top of this, as we mentioned before, loans were difficult to obtain; therefore, it was essential to look for resources in the stock market.

Both the Cablevisión-Multicanal merger and the Group's 2016 spin-off, almost ten years later, had the purpose of obtaining revenue to finance the necessary infrastructure for the offer of cross-media

Economic Profile 79

services. This is evidenced by the different lines of business and their evolution in the Group's share of revenue, where cable TV and internet had much more impact than the other units.

The evolution of Grupo Clarín's lines of business in the 2007–2017 period is illustrated in Figure 14.

Although the period analyzed here is until 2015 (before the Group's spin-off), a broader series is shown at this point, since the Group maintained a single profit and loss statement until 2016. In 2017, Grupo Clarín and CVH began to report profits as separate companies, and the mobile communications line of business was added in 2016, after the acquisition of Nextel. However, despite preparing individual reports, some periods show a consistent series per line of business. This changed significantly after the merger between Cablevisión and Telecom, which can be seen in the annual profits of 2018 and 2019.

As shown in Figure 14, the cable TV and internet segment is the line of business that represents the highest revenue, with a 67 percent average share of revenues over the ten-year period (2007–2017). It initially represented 59.59 percent in 2007 and 2008, and then peaked in 2014 and 2016, when it grew to over 70 percent of the Group's revenues.

Also noteworthy is the fact that this peak occurred during the last two years of the Cristina Fernández de Kirchner administration,

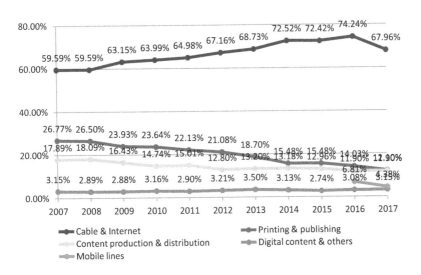

Figure 14 Participation by business line (2007–2017).

which means that public policies aimed at restricting corporate groups and the direct confrontation between the Group and the government were not obstacles to the growth of their most profitable lines of business, as the Group claimed when it accused the government of restricting their freedom of enterprise (Bizberge, 2017). This was emphasized in 2016, when the cable TV and internet segment reached a 74.24 percent share of revenue, during the first year of the presidency of Mauricio Macri, who was very receptive to the Group's demands and interests.

The printing and publishing lines of business (newspapers and magazines) and the content production and distribution lines of business (free-to-air TV and radio) had an average share of revenue of 20 percent and 14 percent, respectively, from 2007 to 2017. Moreover, there is a declining trend in both cases, in contrast to the sustained growth of cable TV and internet services. But this does not mean that the Group had stopped making investments in those areas. The main developments in these lines of business during that period were the transmission and production of HD content in *Canal 13*, the free-to-air TV channel, and in TN, the news channel; investments in the TV series in the ARTEAR study; the development of a big data office for the *Clarín* newspaper; and the creation of an editorial office for print, web and mobile content. Overall, the digital content line represented a 3 percent share of the Group's revenues.

There are no significant changes in this period as regards the Group's concentration of ownership. Following the 2006 Cablevisión-Multicanal merger, this phase marks the consolidation and leadership of the cable TV and internet lines of business against the rest of the lines, and the solid bet on digitization in all business segments.

The general backdrop of this process was a strong confrontation with Fernández de Kirchner's government over the Audiovisual Services Law. Even though this did not impact the size of the Group, it did shake both the stock market and the distribution of profits among shareholders. Regarding the former, the evolution of the Clarín share price shows a steep decline in the stock market from 2009 (after the law was passed) and, primarily between 2011 and 2014 (the same period in which the controversy was taken to court and an attempt was made to adapt to the regulations), as shown in Figure 15.

Economic Profile 81

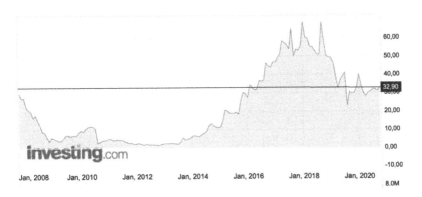

Figure 15 Evolution of Clarín share (2008–2020).

By reviewing the annual closing price of the shares in the London and Buenos Aires stock exchanges, it can be seen in Figure 16 that the highest peaks occurred in 2007 (USD 13.88 in the London Stock Exchange and USD 7.23 in the Buenos Aires stock exchange, according to the Central Bank of Argentina), when the group was initially listed after the Cablevisión-Multicanal merger. Then, there was a peak in the 2015 closing (USD 19.88 in London and USD 16.83 in Buenos Aires), when the administration changed and Macri took office. The upturn at the 2016 closing is even more interesting: The value per share reached USD 25.6 in London and USD 14.01 in Buenos Aires. In both cases, the 2007 value doubled. This dramatic growth coincided with the announcement that the Group would spin off into Grupo Clarín and Cablevisión Holding.

Despite the fact that the 2007, 2015 and 2016 values are revealing, annual data is not always the best option to show market reactions to political events. For instance, when the Supreme Court of Justice ruled that the Audiovisual Communication Services Law was indeed constitutional in October 2013, Clarín's value per share fell almost 21 percent on the London stock market and nearly 6 percent in Buenos Aires. Market quotations were then suspended for the rest of that day. Nonetheless, there was a significant upturn in the company's annual value at the end of 2013 compared to 2012 (USD 5.5 in 2013 versus USD 2.5 in 2012).

82 Economic Profile

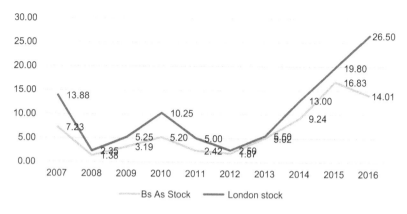

Figure 16 Clarín Group price per share (2007–2016).

The conflict between Fernández de Kirchner's government and Grupo Clarín also impacted the annual distribution of dividends, showing how shareholders organized the business.

Table 2 shows the increase in dividends between 2008 and 2011, followed by a fall between 2013 and 2015 (which is connected to the previous fiscal year and the disputes regarding the implementation of the Audiovisual Services Law), and an upturn in 2016–2017 (annual reports include the results from the previous year).

Generally speaking, the payment of dividends to shareholders has represented 15–30 percent of all revenue earned throughout those years, with three exceptions. During the two years after the Cablevisión-Multicanal merger, there was no distribution of dividends. The first year, this was decided by the shareholders themselves. In 2010, an action brought by Administración Nacional de Seguridad Social (ANSES, the National Social Security Administration) stated that the provision was not valid and demanded payment of its dividends (it had a 9 percent interest in Grupo Clarín's share capital). The third exception was linked to the 2014 profit and loss statement (fiscal year 2013): That year, it reported the lowest results during this period. Therefore, the decision was made to allocate profits partly to the payment of dividends and partly to the creation of a voluntary reserve for the financial aid of subsidiaries and for covering litigation expenses associated with the Audiovisual Services Law. However, this was not limited to that year; between 2012 and 2015, more than half of the profits were used as reserve funds for that purpose, as well as a reserve for future dividends.

The foregoing leads to the conclusion that, even though Grupo Clarín claimed that the law posed a threat to its sustainability (which was dismissed by the Supreme Court), the data reveal that shareholders almost

Table 2 Payment of dividends

	Results	Dividend payment	Legal reserve	Undistributed profits	Other	Comments
2008	85.92	15.43	3.34	48.16	0.36	"Other" corresponds to negative, unallocated results of 2007
2009	83.13		4.16	78.99	NA	General Meeting decided not to pay dividends
2010	136.50	30.69	6.82		NA	No dividends were paid because of ANSES lawsuit
2011	126.46	32.69	5.79	98.98	334.47	Results include unallocated results for the previous year. Totaled 372.88, from which 334.47 in the "Other" column refers to the legal reserve for distribution of future dividends (93.7) for ANSES lawsuit; voluntary reserve for future dividends (72.63) and liquid result (168.12)
2012		32.69				The report states that what was already approved by the Meeting for the previous period was paid
2013	88.01		4.38	0.21	83.39	Unallocated results refer to absorbing negative unallocated results. "Other" corresponds to the voluntary reserve for the financial aid of subsidiaries and media law
2014	59.09	29.56	0.83		28.69	"Other" corresponds to the voluntary reserve for the financial aid of subsidiaries and media law
2015	86.73	26.97			59.76	"Other" corresponds to the voluntary reserve for the financial assistance of subsidiaries and media law
2016	127.47	20.30			107.24	"Other" corresponds to a reserve for future dividends
2017	152.41	28.92			123.49	"Other" is divided half for the reserve for future dividends and the other half for creating a voluntary reserve to ensure the liquidity of the company and its subsidiaries

In millions of dollars, based on BCRA official quotation.

never stopped receiving dividends – despite being moderate in some years, which was made up for in other years. At the same time, this sheds light on the organization of capital in the business in politically adverse times.

Grupo Clarín in 2016–2020: "The First Argentine Holding of Converged Communications"

Macri's communication policies from 2015 favored a scenario in which concentration was deepened under the rhetoric of convergence and competition through regulatory changes that had an immediate effect on the structure and business of Grupo Clarín.

The admission of Fintech (Grupo Clarín's partner in Cablevisión) to Telecom,[24] the subsequent acquisition of Nextel, the Group's spin-off and the merger between Cablevisión and Telecom are all part of the changes that were facilitated during Macri's government.

As opposed to the expansion process in the telecommunications infrastructure area during this period, Grupo Clarín experienced a reduction in its press line not only in terms of revenue, but also because of the February 2017 shutdown of the Arte Gráfico Rioplatense (AGR) printing plant, where the Group's editorial products were previously printed. In November of the same year, the news agency DyN (partnership of *Clarín* and *La Nación*, as well as other newspapers) was shut down and, a month later, the discontinuation of *La Razón*, the free newspaper, was announced. In all three of these cases, the Group claimed that the decisions were based on the crisis that the print media industry was experiencing in the country (and in the world) due to the advent of new technologies. Figure 17 presents Grupo Clarín's fourth expansion stage following these changes.

The spin-off and the merger with Telecom once again show the need to resort to the stock market and to control indebtedness to expand the business. However, this time there was a greater risk due to the increased scale of the company.

At the same time, these changes demonstrate that infrastructure (rather than content) is a key driver for the Group's strategy, and that Cablevisión-Telecom, self-designated as "the first Argentine holding of converged communications," is the leader in that strategy.

In 2018, Telecom announced investments for USD 5 billion for the 2018–2020 period (which would later be minimized because of the economic crisis and the devaluations in the final part of Macri's administration) in order to deploy fiber and 4G mobile network and to boost the online video streaming business (*Clarín*, January 31, 2018). The announcements about these areas, which were deemed critical, are in tune with the significance of the different lines of business in the Group's revenue. As we can see in Figure 17, the main lines after

Economic Profile 85

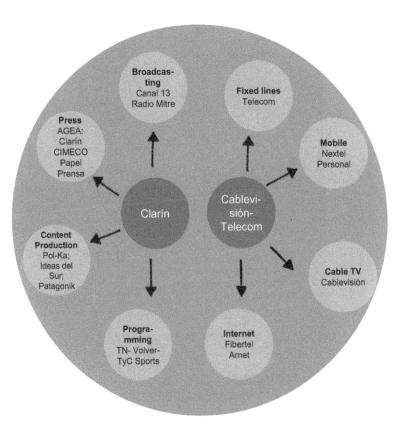

Figure 17 Clarín's fourth phase of expansion (2016–2020).

the merger were cable TV and internet services, to which the mobile communications line was added.

Even though the companies had been making separate profit and loss statements since 2017, the 2018 balance sheet – the first after the merger – included changes due to the new situation of these companies, as well as governmental provisions enabling inflation-adjusted statements. This resulted in considerable modifications regarding the aggregate share of revenue of the different lines of business. This is the reason why the cable TV and internet segment, which used to account for 70 percent of revenues, represented almost 39 percent in 2019. Nevertheless, it is still the most profitable line, followed by mobile communications (which represented 29.23 percent and 31.32 percent in 2018 and 2019, respectively). Meanwhile, the printing and publishing line,

86 Economic Profile

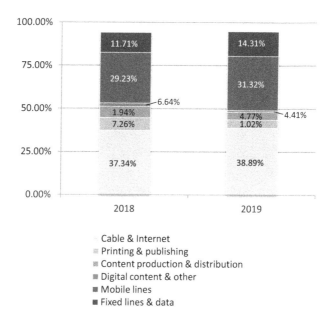

Figure 18 Share per business line (2018–2019).

the content production and distribution line, and the digital content area practically halved their influence.

Once again, this analysis presents aggregate results, while the dollar amounts for each of the business lines are constant compared to previous years, as shown in Table 3.

In mobile communications, the large difference between 2016–2017 and 2018–2019 is due to the fact that, during the first period, the revenue from Nextel was included, whereas the operations from Personal (Telecom) were added later. This is also the case for the fixed telephony business.

The decline in revenue from the production and content distribution line, and the printing and publishing line, is attributed mainly to the decrease in advertising sales in both cases, as well as the decline in the printing and distribution segment. Lastly, the drop in the digital content area is the result of a reduction in sales. In all these cases, it is also necessary to mark variations caused by the exchange rate fluctuation in the Argentine peso and the US dollar, due to devaluation.

At this stage (2016–2020), Grupo Clarín satisfied and surpassed its desire of becoming a key operator and competing with the regional

Table 3 Revenues per business line (2007–2019)

	Total sales	Cable TV and internet	Printing and publishing	Content production and distribution	Digital content and others	Mobile phones	Fixed lines and data
2007	1,409.55	840	377.33	252.22	44.41		
2008	1,815.00	1,081.49	480.98	328.35	52.5		
2009	1,791.00	1,131	428.58	294.24	51.55		
2010	1,952.00	1,249	461.38	287.65	61.6		
2011	2,361.38	1,534.36	522.69	354.41	68.52		
2012	2,487.67	1,670.68	524.33	318.46	79.96		
2013	2,588.38	1,779.03	484.09	341.55	90.53		
2014	2,415.79	1,751.98	373.97	318.51	75.60		
2015	2,998.00	2,171.02	464.23	388.50	82.1		
2016	2,786.07	2,068.42	390.78	331.52	85.8	189.72	
2017	3,319.87	2,256.27	401.75	395.22	104.7	145.36	
2018	7,026.84	2,623.85	509.96	466.52	136.27	2,053.89	822.93
2019	5,436.07	2,113.82	259.27	239.59	55.68	1,702.46	778.00

Source: Own creation based on the companies' public reports. Expressed in millions of dollars (USD). Average annual price based on BCRA. 2007: USD 3.11; 2008: USD 3.16; 2009: USD 3.73; 2010: USD 3.91; 2011: USD 4.13; 2012: USD 4.55; 2013: USD 5.48; 2014: USD 8.12; 2015: USD 9.27; 2016: USD 14.78; 2017: USD 16.6; 2018: USD 28.13; 2019: USD 48.28

telecommunications companies in the local market (Telefónica, Telecom and Claro). In Argentina, Grupo Clarín has beaten them: It is the only conglomerate present in all markets, including media and telecommunications; moreover, it is the number one company in these markets (except in mobile and free-to-air TV, where it is in second place).

To achieve this position of power, which is unique in the region, the Group resorted again to the stock market and controlled indebtedness formula to make new investments. The spin-off had a massive impact on the stock market, and it marked the supremacy of the networks unit over the contents unit. In 2017, when Cablevisión Holding's value per share was USD 22.5, Grupo Clarín's was USD 6. Simultaneously, that difference could also be seen in the overall turnover of each company. While Cablevisión Holding generated net sales of USD 5,973 million (5.9 billion) in 2018 and USD 4,909 million (4.9 billion) in 2019, Clarín's revenue was USD 1,052.9 million (1.052 billion) and USD 526.7 million, respectively.[25]

Despite favorable regulations during Macri's government, the macroeconomic situation (in the context of abrupt devaluation) slowed down the investments that had been announced and affected both the financial results (decrease in revenue and net profit[26]) and the share value, which collapsed.[27] This potentially put the Group in a position similar to the situation it was in after the Cablevisión-Multicanal merger. By reason of the operation and its debts, the amounts of money that were at risk in the merger were higher this time.

New Business Lines and Digital Restructuring

Digital restructuring and multiplatform development are part of Clarín's strategic vision for all business units. Even though the Group affirms that no area within the organizational structure is in charge of that process, they do acknowledge that there is cooperation among the different areas. These matters are discussed at "the digital board," where Pagliaro, one of the shareholders of the Group, is actively engaged. Etchevers, Grupo Clarín's External Communications Manager, stated:

> On a corporate level, the digital strategy is coordinated by the Executive Committee (the shareholders) and the managers from each business unit, as part of the planning and management control process. Moreover, the digital board meets every month and works with one of the shareholders, Lucio Pagliaro, which means

that top management participates in it. The purpose is not only to join efforts, but also to assess performance and to analyze how each of the digital undertakings is working, what can be improved and what we can copy from other units that may be enriching. We begin to see some areas for joint work, where we can certainly add value, as with big data. We are currently exploring the topic of programmatic advertising, which *Clarín* developed really well and is beginning to cover all the programmatic advertising services in other units of the Group. We also have digital subscription strategies and content positioning strategies for social media and platforms. Another aspect that we are analyzing is Flow and *Canal 13*, the development of a product aimed at both business units at the same time... if we can create more value in something in particular, we explore it, but we do not neglect what we have already built in each brand. That's an important asset.

This introduces two main questions: First, the performance of the business model, which is increasingly taking advantage of the data-driven logic and seeks to implement mechanisms that are similar to those used in internet platforms. Second, traditional ideas that characterize the performance of cultural industries are strengthened, which is the case for synergies in the development of economies of scale to lower costs and, with digital convergence, economies of scope.

Another underlying aspect is the development of the online video streaming service as one of Cablevisión-Telecom's biggest bets. With the strength of Grupo Clarín in the distribution of cable TV and broadband, since 2016, the Group has ventured into its own OTT model through Flow, to position itself as an "entertainment supermarket" (Telecom, 2020a).

Flow is a platform that includes the Group's traditional channels as well as original productions created in partnership with different production companies (some released exclusively, and others also broadcast in free-to-air and pay TV). In 2019, it enabled access through its interface to Netflix, YouTube and Disney+, the video streaming services, and it planned to include the Amazon Prime Video App as well. As of the second quarter of 2020, it had 1.07 million subscribers and a total of 3.5 million cable TV customers, 5 million connected devices and 22 original productions that it co-produced (Hernández, October 1, 2020; Telecom, 2020b). However, the share of revenue generated by Flow is still a minority portion of the subscription video on demand (SVOD) market, which is led by Netflix (+80 percent of the market) and followed far behind by Amazon.

Carlos Moltini, former CEO of Cablevisión and current Chair of the Board at Telecom, shared the following during a press conference:

> Flow is at the core of our strategy... In our view, Flow is an entertainment supermarket... We believe that Flow has to be the main entertainment experience in people's lives and we cannot limit ourselves to what we are capable of distributing.
> (Crettaz, February 16, 2019)

Therefore, Flow represents a new business opportunity for the company to reposition itself not only in content production, but also as an intermediary (aggregator) for content distribution in the digital world. For this purpose, the Group forms strategic alliances to include its competitors – global players who are leaders in digital content consumption. It is also considering partnerships with the Group's own cell phone businesses, with zero rating offers for the company's clients.[28] Likewise, the developments with Flow involve new projects, such as artificial intelligence tests for e-Sports and gaming experiences (iProUP, January 6, 2020).

In a world where a large portion of the consumption of cultural material happens on the internet, Grupo Clarín understood that, in order to maintain its leadership position with the new global players (most of them from the United States), it needed to re-intermediate people's conditions of access and the way in which content is spread within its own ecosystem, and this ecosystem should not be entirely closed. That way, not only does *Clarín* "resist," but it also designs a "proactive" strategy that includes global audiovisual service providers to support its undisputed leadership in Argentina.

Seventy-Five Years of Grupo Clarín

Throughout its history, but mainly since the 1990s, *Clarín* focused its growth strategy on controlled indebtedness and ongoing reinvestment within the communications sector. It also knew how to adapt to changes in the media business and implemented a solid strategy for the growth of telecom networks.

Clarín was born as a newspaper, and then continued with radio and TV to be present in the content generation space; afterward, it turned to the infrastructure area for digital convergence. For the last 25 years, it has been aspiring to become a telecommunications company. Even though having a "voice" in different formats gave it the power of political influence – the latent threat of conflict with anything that may put its plans at risk – its dominant position in the telecom networks space gave it economic power to become a key player in the landscape of converged communications.

In this regard, in connection with the repeated phrase "content is king," we can observe the central position gained by distribution networks and the capacity to re-intermediate the conditions to access content in the digital world. That is something that *Clarín* has understood, and has deployed an aggressive strategy to that end, combining elements of traditional media management and telecom network economics.

In the period of multimedia expansion, the number of subscribers to its cable service allowed Clarín to secure financing in the stock market, and the growth levels after the spin-off and the merger with Telecom have renewed those opportunities. Despite the fact that, at this stage, the sales volume increases the risk, this same volume may also provide the scale and audacity that it needs to compete outside Argentine borders.

Notes

1. This 71 percent is broken down as follows: 29.8 percent is owned by Magnetto; 24.85 percent is owned by Marcela Noble and 24.85 percent by Felipe Noble; 10.3 percent is owned by Aranda and 10.22 percent is owned by Pagliaro (RSF and *Tiempo Argentino*, 2019).
2. The Board of Directors of Cablevisión Holding and Grupo Clarín comprise ten regular members and ten alternate members each.
3. He was a member of the Board of Grupo Clarín and of the Surveillance Committee of Papel Prensa.
4. Partner of the well-known namesake law firm. Between 2018 and 2019, he was a member of the Board of Telecom Argentina. Additionally, he was listed as a minority shareholder when Arte Radiotelevisivo Argentino (ARTEAR) was established as the Group's company through which Grupo Clarín accessed broadcast TV station *Canal 13* in 1989.
5. Member of the Board since 1999. He is the External Relations Director of Grupo Clarín.
6. José Antonio Aranda's brother.
7. Collaborator of David Martínez. Additionally, from 2006 onward, he was his representative on the Board of Cablevisión, which was later acquired by Grupo Clarín.
8. He joined Grupo Clarín in 1990, first as CFO, then as General Manager of Multicanal. He took part in the Multicanal-Cablevisión merger in 2006.
9. Lawyer representing Grupo Clarín.
10. He held leadership positions in Clarín (Business Development Manager) and Multicanal (COO for International Operations).
11. He holds the position of independent director. He has served on the Telecom Board since 2016, when David Martínez was authorized to join the company.

12 With the arrival of Martínez to Telecom in 2016, he had been appointed CEO for Telecom, and was then replaced with Moltini.
13 He had held the position of CEO at Procter & Gamble, and previously CEO of TIM Brazil (an affiliate of Telecom Italy). He was Head of Mobile at Telecom Italy.
14 He joined Telecom Argentina's Board in 2016, after the government authorized David Martínez to join Telecom.
15 Broadcast TV station *Canal 13* and pay TV stations TN (news channel), *Quiero Música* (music channel), *Sports* (sports channel), *Volver, Magazine* and *Metro* (general-affairs channels).
16 Broadcast TV station *Telefé*, pay TV stations MTV and VH1 (music channels) and *Nickelodeon* and *Comedy Central*.
17 Broadcast TV station *América TV* and news channel A24.
18 The average foreign exchange rate in 1945 was 1 USD – 4 $AR (BCRA).
19 The company, initially belonging to national entrepreneur Eduardo Eurnekian (the owner of Corporación América and the license holder of Argentine Airports), was transferred to the US company TCI in 1995 and then to the CEI-Telefónica pair in 1998. Between 2000 and 2006, Cablevisión was managed by the investment fund HTM&F, which in 2006 sold its shareholdings to Grupo Clarín.
20 The Cultural Asset and Heritage Preservation Law (Law 25750 of 2003), which allowed for foreign capital to be involved in cultural industries with a 30 percent cap, prevented Clarín from being acquired by its creditors in the face of financial difficulties caused by the end of the peso-dollar parity system and the devaluation that followed the political, economic and social crisis of 2001. Another key measure was Decree 527/2005, which, also in connection to the economic crisis, cancelled the lapsing of broadcasting licenses for ten years.
21 As mentioned, in 1997 Grupo Clarín partnered with CEI-Telefónica to acquire VCC, which until then was one of the main cable TV systems in Argentina, alongside Multicanal and Cablevisión (then belonging to Telefónica).
22 Interviewed by the authors on September 28, 2020.
23 Interviewed by the authors on September 28, 2020.
24 David Martínez, through Fintech, obtained authorization – which had previously been denied by the Fernández de Kirchner administration – to join Telecom. He held a 68 percent equity interest in Sofora (at that time, the controlling company of Telecom Argentina, through Nortel Inversora), and then acquired 32 percent from Grupo Werthein, thus acquiring 100 percent of Telecom Argentina.
25 Original figures were stated in Argentine pesos. For Cablevisión Holding, net sales were AR$ 168,046 million in 2018, and AR$ 237,024 million in 2019. For Grupo Clarín, sales were AR$ 29,619 million in 2018 and AR$ 526.69 million in 2019. The conversion to US dollars was made using the BCRA rate for the respective years.
26 For Cablevisión-Telecom, the losses amounted to USD 107.4 million in 2019 (AR$ 5.18 billion) for the drop in total sales across all service lines, compared to the positive results of 2018, when the net profit amounted to USD 102.4 (AR$ 2.88 billion). Whereas in Grupo Clarín, losses amounted to USD 30.21 million in 2019 (AR$ 1.45 billion) compared to USD 48.24

in 2018 (AR$ 1.35 billion), mainly due to the drop in gross revenue in the Content Production & Distribution segment (broadcast TV).
27 The value of the Cablevisión Holding share went down from USD 22.5 in 2016, to USD 5.8 in 2018 and USD 3.5 in 2019. The value of the Grupo Clarín share went down from USD 6 in 2016 to USD 1.89 in 2019 (reference value: London Stock Exchange).
28 In December 2019, *Flow Pass*, a zero rating offering, was launched. Through this offering, Personal mobile customers with 5 GB and 8 GB subscriptions were given access to Flow contents without data consumption (up to 10 GB) for 30 days. The company had already tried this type of practice in 2018, when it made available to its Cablevisión Flow subscribers non-competitive soccer matches that the Argentine team played after the World Cup, the Libertadores Cup finals between Boca and River teams and the 2018 Soccer Clubs Cup, without consuming Personal mobile data.

References

Albornoz, Luis (Coord.) (2000). *Al fin solos. La nueva televisión del Mercosur*. Buenos Aires: Editorial Ciccus- La Crujía.

Albornoz, Luis and Pablo Hernández (2005). "La radiodifusión en Argentina entre 1995 y 1999: concentración, desnacionalización y ausencia de control público", in Mastrini, G. (ed.) *Mucho ruido, pocas leyes. Economía y política de comunicación en la Argentina (1920–2004)* (pp. 257–286). Buenos Aires: La Crujía.

Becerra, Martín and Guillermo Mastrini (2017). *La concentración infocomunicacional en América Latina (2000–2015). Nuevos medios y tecnologías, menos actores*. Bernal: UNQ –OBSERVACOM.

Bizberge, Ana (2015). "Los modelos de negocio de la televisión en internet en el mercado latinoamericano". *Austral Comunicación*, 4(1), 83–125. https://doi.org/10.26422/aucom.2015.0401.biz

Bizberge, Ana (2017). "El impacto de la regulación en el desarrollo de la convergencia digital: El caso de Clarín y el rol de las telefónicas". *Austral Comunicación*, 6(1), 107–132. https://doi.org/10.26422/aucom.2017.0601.biz

Bizberge, Ana (2019). *Alcances y desafíos de la convergencia digital y su impacto para la elaboración de políticas de comunicación. Un estudio de la convergencia regulatoria en Argentina, Brasil y México (2000–2017)*. Thesis for the PhD in Social Sciences. University of Buenos Aires (UBA) School of Social Sciences.

Bizberge, Ana (September 1, 2020). "Telcos: altos niveles de concentración derrumban el mito de la competencia". *LetraP*. https://www.letrap.com.ar/nota/2020-9-1-18-28-0-telcos-altos-niveles-de-concentracion-derrumban-el-mito-de-la-competencia

Borrelli, Marcelo and Jorge Saborido (2013). "Por una dictadura desarrollista: el periódico Clarín frente a la política económica del último gobierno de facto en Argentina (1976–1981)", en *StudiaHistorica. Historia Contemporánea* n°31, Universidad de Salamanca, 195–218. https://revistas.usal.es/index.php/0213-2087/article/view/14598/15052

Cablevisión (April 30, 2020). *Annual and Extraordinary Shareholders Meeting of April 29, 2020.* https://www.cablevisionholding.com/files/Comunicados-Prensa/2020/CVH.%20Nota%20CNV%20SINTESIS%20Asamblea%2030-04-20.pdf

Clarín (May 4, 2020). *General Shareholders Meeting of April 30, 2020.* https://grupoclarin.com/IR/files//Comunicados-Prensa/2020/GCSA%20-%20%20SINTESIS%20Asamblea%2031-12-2019%20.pdf

Clarín (January 31, 2018). "Telecom anuncia una inversión de US$ 5.000 millones para mejorar las redes y la conectividad". *Diario Clarín.* https://www.clarin.com/economia/empresas-y-negocios/telecom-anuncia-inversion-us-000-millones-mejorar-redes-conectividad_0_HktGMakIG.html

Crettaz, José (February 1, 2019). Carlos Moltini: "Flow es un supermercado del entretenimiento que incluirá a Netflix, Amazon Video, Disney+ y todo lo que surja". https://josecrettaz.com/telecomunicaciones/carlos-moltini-flow-es-un-supermercado-del-entretenimiento-que-incluira-netflix-amazon-prime-disney-y-todo-lo-que-surja/

Cronista (January 7, 2020). "Roberto Nobile asumió como CEO de Telecom Argentina". https://www.cronista.com/apertura-negocio/empresas/Roberto-Nobile-asumio-como-CEO-de-Telecom-Argentina-20200106-0006.html

Espada, Agustín and Santiago Marino (October 11, 2020). "Publicidad oficial gestión Fernández: ganadores, avances y dilemas". *LetraP.* https://www.letrap.com.ar/nota/2020-10-11-9-4-0-publicidad-oficial-gestion-fernandez-ganadores-avances-y-dilemas

Grupo Clarín (2007). *Annual Report 2007.* https://grupoclarin.com/IR/files//Annual-Report/reporte-anual-2007.pdf

Grupo Clarín. *Annual Reports and Consolidated Financial Statements, 2008–2019.*

Hernández, Gustavo (October 1, 2020). "Flow de Cablevisión llega a 22 producciones originales con el estreno de Post Mortem." TAVI Latam. https://www.tavilatam.com/argentina-flow-de-cablevision-llega-a-22-producciones-originales-con-el-estreno-de-post-mortem/?utm_source=newsletter&utm_medium=email&utm_campaign=tavi_latam_global_google_presento_un_nuevo_chromecast_con_control_remoto_y_sistema_operativo_propio&utm_term=2020-10-01

Infobae (May 21, 2020). "Carlos Moltini es el nuevo Presidente del Directorio de Telecom Argentina." https://www.infobae.com/economia/networking/2020/05/21/carlos-moltini-es-el-nuevo-presidente-del-directorio-de-telecom-argentina/

iProUP (January 6, 2020). "Nobile asume como CEO de Telecom y termina el 'doble comando': cuál es la estrategia para que la empresa crezca más rápido." https://www.iproup.com/innovacion/10355-nobile-asume-como-ceo-de-telecom-y-pone-a-flow-como-estrategia-de-crecimiento

López, José (2008). *El hombre de Clarín. Vida pública y privada de Héctor Magnetto.* Buenos Aires: Sudamericana.

Marino, Santiago (2017). *Políticas de comunicación del sector audiovisual modelos divergentes, resultados equivalentes. La televisión por cable y el cine en la Argentina (1989–2007).* Bernal: Universidad Nacional de Quilmes.

Mastrini, Guillermo (2013). *Las industrias culturales en Argentina: Economía y política del sector audiovisual en la década del '90.* Doctoral Thesis, Universidad Complutense de Madrid School of Information Sciences.

Mastrini, Guillermo and Martín Becerra (2006). *Periodistas y Magnates. Estructura y concentración de las industrias culturales en América Latina.* Buenos Aires: Prometeo Libros.

Mochkofsky, Graciela (2011). *Pecado original. Clarín, los Kirchner y la lucha por el poder.* Buenos Aires: Planeta.

Postolski, Glenn and Santiago Marino (2005). "Relaciones peligrosas: los medios y la dictadura. Entre el control, la censura y los negocios", in Mastrini, G. (ed.). *Mucho ruido, pocas leyes. Economía y política de comunicación en la Argentina (1920–2004)* (pp. 155–184). Buenos Aires: La Crujía.

Sinclair, J. (1999). *Latin American Television. A Global View.* New York: Oxford University Press.

Sivak, Martín (2013). *Clarín. Una historia.* Buenos Aires: Planeta.

Sivak, Martín (2015). *Clarín. La era Magnetto.* Buenos Aires: Planeta.

Telecom (May 12, 2016). "El Grupo Telecom designó nuevo CEO y equipo directivo". https://institucional.telecom.com.ar/prensa/notas/2016-05-12/designacion-nuevo-ceo-y-equipo.html

Telecom (2020a). *Company Presentation, March 2020.* https://institucional.telecom.com.ar/data/repo/Telecom%20Argentina%20Presentation%204Q19%20.pdf

Telecom (2020b). *Company Presentation, August 2020.* https://institucional.telecom.com.ar/data/repo/Telecom%20Argentina%20Presentation%202Q20esp.pdf

Tiempo Argentino and RSF (2019). *Monitoreo de la Propiedad de los Medios de Argentina.* https://argentina.mom-rsf.org/es/

Interview

Interview with Martín Etchevers, External Communications Manager, Grupo Clarín. September 28, 2020.

4 Cultural Profile of *Clarín*

Introduction

As the largest cross-media conglomerate in Argentina, Grupo Clarín is active in the whole range of cultural services offered in the country. As discussed in the previous chapters, it started as a newspaper 75 years ago, focusing on popular segments and the grassroots, and gradually expanding the range of its readership. Although currently the Group regards itself as a diversified company, for many years *Clarín* was considered the newspaper of the urban middle classes with relevant informative and cultural content. In Argentina, these sectors reached their summit between 1960 and 1990. After 1989, when *Clarín* turned into a cross-media group through the acquisition of radio and television stations, the company's cultural profile remained the same, as opposed to other options with more popular content.

Well into the 21st century, a number of factors, including its expansion into markets including pay television and internet service provision, the open confrontation with the Cristina Fernández de Kirchner administrations – dubbed by one of the chief editors as "war journalism" – and the decline in sales of audiovisual and print products, led to the editorial department losing influence in the Group and becoming subordinate to the business growth strategy.

To analyze the cultural profile of Grupo Clarín for this chapter, the definition of scholar Jorge Rivera, who was also an outstanding columnist in the culture section of the newspaper, has been used:

> All journalism is, in short, a "cultural" phenomenon, due to its origins, objectives and procedures, but historically the name of "cultural journalism" has been applied to a very complex and heterogeneous sector of media, genres and products that, for creative, critical, reproductive or informative purposes, deal with the fields of "fine arts," the "belles-lettres," currents of thought, social and human sciences, the so-called Argentine popular culture, and

many other aspects that have to do with the production, circulation and consumption of symbolic goods (...).
(Rivera, 1995: 19)

Thus, Grupo Clarín has been studied as a cultural phenomenon in its entirety, but at the same time focusing on specific references to the readership and the radio and television audience that the company has sought to develop. In previous chapters, the history of Grupo Clarín was segmented in terms of its economic growth or its negotiations with different governments. In this chapter, the basis for segmentation will be the notion of culture that predominated in the newspaper. The cultural history of Grupo Clarín can be broken down into five periods: (1) between 1945 and 1969, a leading role was taken by the newspaper's founder, Roberto Noble, who was committed to an idea of agile and popular culture that was, in turn, associated with a steady increase in sales; (2) the period between 1969 and 1982 was informed by the idea of culture promoted by Rogelio Frigerio and was based on national development in conjunction with a global geopolitical vision; (3) between 1982 and 2001, we note that culture was subordinated to a business criteria that allowed for economic expansion and the consolidation of a culturally diversified group; (4) between 2001 and 2009, Grupo Clarín had to revamp its damaged economic status and therefore assumed a cultural profile more closely linked with national activities; and (5) in recent years, due to the strong confrontations with the Cristina Fernández de Kirchner administrations, the target audience was redefined. Cultural approaches have also been accompanied by a marked ideological bias. Furthermore, the digitization of cultural markets is also a relevant aspect of this last stage.

1945–1969: The Noble Era

Unlike most Latin American capitals, Buenos Aires had a significant number of newspapers and periodicals in the mid-1940s when *Clarín* newspaper was launched. As a result of the early schooling of the popular urban classes, newspaper reading levels were quite high for a peripheral country. In more general terms, there was room for the development of cultural projects linked to the popular classes.

The historian Roy Hora (2020) gives an accurate account of the production and circulation of cultural assets in the first half of the 20th century:

> In those years, the Argentine culture accentuated its democratic character. Newspapers such as *Crítica*, but also radio and cinema,

were the means through which many cultural expressions became a part of the everyday lives in the majority of Argentine households, denying or challenging the hierarchies of power and prestige typical of the upper classes and groups endowed with greater cultural capital. This was also the time of emergence of popular, self-made heroes who owed nothing to the patronage of the political or cultural elites, very visible in areas such as sports, the racetrack or the entertainment industry. (...) It is needless to subscribe in all detail to the theory that the narratives of conflict between rich and poor offered by the radio and the cinema screen expressed the maturity of a popular anti-elitist and rebellious culture, to agree that, already in the 1930s, Argentine culture was permeated with an intense plebeian tone.

Argentine popular culture was in a state of flux, as described by Hora, making it easier to picture the audience that a new newspaper could target in 1945. Even more so, if one considers that after the death of its founder Natalio Botana in 1941, the newspaper *Crítica*,[1] which had developed great political impact in previous decades, had gone into a slow decline from which it would never recover.

Roberto Noble, whose express aspiration was to influence politics, knew that the newspaper should reach out to the popular classes. While it adopted a tabloid format that was easy to read on public transport, it also dissociated itself from the yellow press. The newspaper was intended for the popular classes who were interested in the daily life of an ever-expanding city in which they could aspire to thrive. From 1945 onward, these segments of society had greater participation in the country's political life.

Sivak (2013) emphasizes that

> Noble wanted a massive newspaper, light on ideology, that would influence the greatest number of Argentines and project his own figure. (...) *Clarín* became the extension of that man. He lent to the newspaper his ideological flexibility, his capacity to grasp the atmosphere of the period, his skills as a political negotiator, and his eagerness for social advancement.

A self-congratulatory statement by Grupo Clarín maintained that

> *Clarín* is inspired by the English *Daily Mirror*, with a clear and straightforward narrative style to present the news, and

user-friendly language with well-structured, polished writing. The pages did not focus only on the hard sections of economics or politics.

(López, 2008)

This view is enhanced from a social perspective by the writer Osvaldo Bayer (2003) – the founder of the Culture and Nation supplement in 1969 – when he noted that Noble stood out for continuing the sharpness of Botana in *Crítica*, with popular language, journalists who reported on daily life in the city and a bohemian style. As in different opportunities throughout its history, a combination of opportunism and business savvy enabled *Clarín* to slowly fill the void left by *Crítica*. To facilitate this move, Noble hired several journalists from *Crítica*, which was struggling to pay wages.

As described in the political profile in Chapter 2, the newspaper targeted a popular lower-middle class that did not necessarily identify with the newspaper's editorial line, but rather with its ability to interpret and report the challenges of their daily lives. It should be recalled that during the first Peronist period[2] (1946–1955), there was an expansion of domestic demand as a result of the exponential increase in workers' purchasing power especially in the period between 1946 and 1949.

The newspaper included many stories about the rank and file, in which lower and lower-middle classes could see themselves. Those stories were short and reader-friendly; at the same time, one could appreciate the careful writing. During this first stage (1945–1969), the paper relied on outstanding cultural referents, including Raúl González Tuñón, Hamlet Lima Quintana, Haroldo Conti and Tito Cossa; intellectuals such as Juan Carlos Portantiero and Félix Luna; journalists like Bernardo Neustadt; and even future owners of other newspapers such as Jacobo Timerman, Héctor Ricardo García and Julio Ramos.

Among the different sections of the newspaper, Sports and Entertainment played a key role from the beginning. Blanca Rébori,[3] journalist at the newspaper between 1967 and 1976, points out that the world of show business took up most of the Art and Shows section, with an overwhelming presence of cinema and theater. There was also a literary supplement that was not aimed at a specific type of reader. This vision coincides with that of Sivak,[4] who argues that the Noble culture was marked by the world of show business. And "show" here was understood as theater – with some radio and *porteño* theater, which was very much related to the private world of Noble's personal tastes. Sivak adds that Sports and Entertainment were central to that broad readership that Noble had in mind, partly following the model of *Crítica*.

In 1954, toward the end of the Peronist government, *Clarín* had consolidated sales of 200,000 copies per day (Sivak, 2013) and had managed to increase its advertising revenues, especially from its classified ads. The fall of Peronism implied a disruption in the editorial line, but at the same time there was continuity in soft content, such as sports and shows. As Sivak noted,

> the abrupt changes of rejection-support-condemnation of Peronism never made *Clarín* lose readers, as proven by the 20 percent increase in the number of copies sold between 1955 and 1956. Ideological coherence does not seem to have been a determining factor, as *Clarín*'s readers were looking for light material. They could easily assimilate the Director's change of clothes.
>
> (Sivak, 2013: 118)

After two military governments, in 1958 Arturo Frondizi (1958–1962)[5] was elected president. He belonged to the Intransigent branch of the Radical Civic Union Party (UCRI), which had agreed to be supported by Perón (whose party was banned). In the UCRI, besides Frondizi, the figure of Rogelio Frigerio stood out. Noble's agenda was so much in harmony with both leaders that the newspaper was identified for decades as an editorial ally of the Frondizi-Frigerism movement. Sivak (2013) points out that during Frondicism, *Clarín*'s position was to defend such a movement, without being overtly partisan, and maintaining its editorial independence.

The relationship with Frondicism is essential in any analysis of the Clarín conglomerate because of the political, economic and cultural implications. As discussed in more detail in the next section, Frigerio had a different idea of culture, much less frivolous than Noble's. But it would take ten years for this new vision to solidify.

Frondizi and Frigerio used the magazine *Qué* as a means of dissemination. The publication enjoyed great success at the time due to its journalistic innovation as well as its aesthetic qualities. It featured columns by well-known intellectuals such as Ernesto Sábato, Arturo Jauretche and Raúl Scalabrini Ortiz. Horacio González[6] points out that this weekly paper, which was among the readings of the popular classes, can be regarded as a precedent for *Clarín*'s Culture and Nation supplement.

Meanwhile, *Clarín* continued to gain readers and grew thanks to government incentives and loans. In the mid-sixties, it exceeded

300,000 copies and became one of the leading Argentine newspapers in terms of sales.

In January 1969, Noble died and his widow, Ernestina Herrera, became the newspaper's General Director. Since the new director lacked experience as an executive or a journalist, she entrusted the management of the newspaper to Frigerio, following the advice of her late husband.

1969–1982: Developmentalism, a National View of Culture

Noble's succession was not free of conflicts and tensions. Although the command remained in the hands of Ernestina Herrera de Noble, she, in turn, delegated it to Frigerio. He was an intellectual trained in the Marxist tradition, who had become an influential politician, a man of power. Dictating the editorial line of a newspaper with a large circulation and high penetration in the popular and middle classes opened up an opportunity for him that he was not going to waste.

Although at that time the editorial staff of *Clarín* included many journalists and politicians directly linked to Frigerio, he did not hold an actual position on the editorial board. On the other hand, the newspaper never really served as the house organ of Frondizi-Frigerism[7] despite its influence and maintained its diverse coverage of topics.

But Frigerio had a concept of culture that he promoted in the paper. In a conference on national culture, he argued,

> The current, generally accepted concept of culture is that of the action of humans on nature and on themselves, modifying themselves and changing their external context with the tools at their disposal, in a given field and environment (...), which field and environment are not universal but national; they become universal as the sum of individual realities, as the acceptance and adaptation of material instruments and ideals.
>
> (1976: 8)

On another occasion, he defined culture as "a category that encompasses, integrates and harmonizes in its universality all regions, social groups, economic activities and ideological or political orientations. The national state is, in turn, the political structure that presides over unity and is thus expressed" (Frigerio, 1968: 15).

In both cases, the national character of culture is stressed, as well as the importance of the state in the development of culture. With the growth of Frigerism, this new vision and culture was given more prominence in the paper. From Noble's somewhat frivolous conception of culture as everyday arts and shows, there was a move to a more comprehensive and profound understanding in this new phase.

Not coincidentally, it was in 1969 when *Clarín* launched the Culture and Nation supplement, which would be part of the newspaper's life for 30 years. Its first director was the left-leaning writer and journalist Osvaldo Bayer, who was ousted from the political scene by Frigerism (he was editorial secretary of the political section), and in his own words was given an "embassy" in the cultural supplement. The journalist Blanca Rébori, one of the very few women who worked at the newspaper at that time, participated in the launch of the supplement. Bayer was in charge of the supplement until 1973, the year in which Frigerism took over the weekly supplement.

According to Rébori, they had been asked to produce a cultural supplement that would include the words "Nation" and "Culture" in the title, and they decided to combine them. In this new space, the newspaper welcomed debates in sociology, anthropology and literary criticism, as well as political and cultural discussions. It represented a new level of openness compared to the literary supplement that had been conceived in Noble's time, which, according to Rébori,[8] had a stagnant vision of culture. Bayer (2003) claims that under his direction, he tried to adopt a federal approach to culture, giving visibility to culture in inner cities, and Rébori emphasizes that it was their goal to promote progressive ideas in a context of strong cultural debate: the 1960–1976 period in Argentina.

Although Developmentalism had been a driving force for the supplement, Rébori points out that both she and Bayer had ample freedom to raise issues and choose their collaborators. At that time, the supplement was assembled on the basis of the collaborations requested by those in charge. Rébori recalls that the supplement was soon appreciated by the cultural community and that it had great impact on radio and other media.

After 1973, the Culture and Nation supplement came to be directly controlled by people who reported to Frigerio. One of the first to be in charge was poet Eduardo Calamaro[9] who, like Frigerio, had been a member of the Communist Party and was later involved with Developmentalism. As a journalist, he had been a member of the founding group of *Qué* magazine. According to Horacio González, in this period a view of a federal national culture gained ground, which even made its way to the pages of *Humor* magazine, with the introduction of a group of Argentine cartoonists who would eventually reach great popularity, and whose work replaced the classic cartoons of the North American cartoonists' union.

In the first half of the 1970s, 25 years after its creation, *Clarín* was already one of Argentina's best-selling newspapers. Its readership, initially formed by the popular classes, expanded to the middle classes, which had reported enormous growth between 1945 and 1975 with the unprecedented participation of salaried workers in the distribution of income, something never seen before or since.

The first years of the 70s were particularly turbulent with military dictatorships and coups d'état, the outlawing of the electoral majority, state intervention in unions and associations, growing political violence and armed organizations. In 1973, Perón won the elections again after 18 years of proscription, but his term of office was very brief, as he died in mid-1974. The tensions of the time were reflected in the editorial department of *Clarín*. Journalists linked to the armed organizations wrote for the paper, and after the 1976 military coup, several journalists who contributed to the newspaper were kidnapped and disappeared.[10]

On the cultural level, there are several who agree that the paper maintained an open perspective, even greater than that on economy, politics or opinion. Albino Gómez,[11] director of the Culture Supplement in those years, admits that he was appointed by Frigerio, but claims that he worked with total freedom. He emphasized the openness of the supplement, in terms of both its stories and the profile of collaborators. The six-page Culture and Nation supplement had a strong reputation, and, under his direction, national topics and authors were featured.

In 1975, there was a change in the Editorial Board that was a turning point in the history of the newspaper. Marcos Cytrynblum took over as Secretary General, giving an even more popular orientation to journalistic coverage, and eventually consolidated *Clarín*'s clear lead in sales.

Then, in March 1976, a coup d'état led to the bloodiest dictatorship in Argentine history. From its editorial line, the newspaper was supportive of the coup. In fact, it was much less critical of the authoritarianism of dictator Jorge Videla than of that of constitutional president Cristina Fernández de Kirchner decades later. Not only was the coverage uncritical of the military government, the newspaper became a partner of the dictatorship by participating in the Papel Prensa company.

The influence of Frigerism was particularly strong in its editorial line and economic section. In this last area, some criticisms of the ultra-liberal conduct of the military government had appeared over the years because it was in clear contradiction to the Developmentalist ideology.

But the newspaper had lost its edge. With the arrival of Cytrynblum, new impetus was given to the sports and entertainment sections, which now occupied more space on the front page. *Clarín*'s sales continued to grow with this casual and popular style. According to Sivak,[12] for Cytrynblum, "Frigerists were not interested in culture. Their sensitivity was not there." In his book on *Clarín*, Sivak (2013: 314) adds that the paper's hyper focus on sports began as a necessity, as a result of censorship and self-censorship, and was definitely established when sales grew exponentially.

In the cultural sector, Guillermo Ariza was in charge of the Culture and Nation supplement between 1977 and 1981, taking the head position at the suggestion of Frigerio. Ariza,[13] a member of the group that was closest to the Developmentalist leader, argues that for Frigerio the "cultural question" was key to the Developmentalist's doctrine. He recalls that Frigerio did not tell him what to write, but made observations when the publication was released. According to Ariza, the world of culture was divided in segments for Frigerio and each one acted as if it were the entire thing, even though all made up the whole. The secret lay in managing them all. In terms of culture, Ariza states that he did not have instructions to create a Developmentalist newspaper, but rather to create the best Spanish-language newspaper, and finally adds that he had to design a cultural supplement for the enlightened sectors who did not read *Clarín*. It was with that objective in mind that he invited the great Argentinean writer Jorge Luis Borges to collaborate with the newspaper. Borges became associated with a historical figure of Developmentalism, Ernesto Sábato.

The Culture section remained open to sociological and philosophical debates that were not an issue of concern for the government. Toward the end of the dictatorship, there was greater openness, and opportunities arose for featuring personalities such as Joan Manuel Serrat or Gabriel García Márquez, both referents of progressive culture. A few years before in August 1979, the newspaper had published an article written by María Elena Walsh that gained publicity because it provided a serious critique of the censorship that the dictatorship imposed on cultural creators. However, there was one caveat: in the same article, the author thanked the military for their actions outside of the cultural scene.

In 1982, two key changes occurred. On the one hand, the defeat in the Malvinas/Falklands War marked the beginning of the end for the dictatorship, and this process culminated in the elections that saw Raúl Alfonsín installed as president in 1983. But, on the other hand, an internal change began when the Director, Herrera de Noble, and the CEO, Magnetto, decided to sever the Developmentalists from the newspaper and the company adopted an economic growth business model.

Eventually, the culture section began to lose consistency. The Developmentalist era can be understood as a period that contributed to consolidating the importance of culture for the newspaper, which, in turn, implied the promotion of national culture in a sort of moderate cultural nationalism. In Ariza's view, this meant that it had a national, integrating vision.

1982–2001: The Consolidation of the Cross-Media Conglomerate

Since Magnetto took over the absolute leadership of *Clarín*, though Noble's widow formally held the Group's chair, the company reoriented its strategy to focus on growth in the media industry. After having positioned *Clarín* as the country's best-selling newspaper, and having dominated the classified ads and advertising market, while ensuring the supply of low-cost paper with Papel Prensa, Magnetto understood that the Group's future depended on its expansion into other media segments. Radio and television were the first objectives, although this goal was not achieved in the short term.

Sivak reports on this process: "For a second phase of expansion, the Group needed to move away from Frigerism and follow criteria of economic efficiency. It goes back to Noble's premise: a non-ideological and fluctuating newspaper" (2013: 372). This situation is presented in a positive light in books written by and for Magnetto's management. José Ignacio López points out that "Magnetto knew how to place *Clarín* in the new era. He took over Radio Mitre and then ventured into the world of telecommunications. The newspaper served as the flagship brand to homogenize the company" (2008).

While *Clarín* was the brand that funded the expansion into other companies and media, allowing the corporation to gain political influence, the leap into new media gradually pushed the newspaper itself aside, both economically and symbolically. Magnetto notes,

> *Clarín*'s growth was basically due to the acceptance of its products and its business strategy. Our expansion strategy was due, first of all, to our editorial results. In fact, without the success of the newspaper, radio, broadcast TV and cable TV, the expansion would have been cut short.
>
> (Magnetto, 2016: 129)

The detachment from Frigerism led the newspaper's products to be reoriented toward the logic of profit maximization. For Ariza, culture became an ornament, while Jorge Aulicino[14] detects a certain eclecticism in the cultural perspective, which varied according to the interests of the market.

However, two distinct sub-stages can be identified within this period. First, the continuity of Cytrynblum as Editorial Secretary, but without the presence of the Developmentalists (1982–1990). Second, the appointment of Roberto Guareschi to that position (1990–2003). What is a common thread for both, beyond the differences that will be addressed later, is that this entire period was determined by the logic of cross-media growth and the newspaper was no longer the only Grupo Clarín product visible to Argentinian society.

As Sivak[15] notes, one can observe

> a period of continuing inertia until Guareschi's injected a modernizing impulse and there was new involvement in the Culture section. There was a long transition from post-Frigerism, and then a gap in the 1980s. There is much continuity with Noble's line in Cytrynblum, in terms of the importance given to sports and shows.

Meanwhile, Ariza[16] has a critical stance on these changes:

> This took place in the context of the hybridization of the newspaper as a medium and the decision to make it a key component of the business plan. They even eliminated the editorials that, since the times of Noble, had been a sacred and prestigious section. A business model where 'culture' embellishes but does not inspire.

Journalist Omar Lavieri[17] states that during this period the newspaper was aimed at the middle class that posted and consumed classified ads, while the newspaper tended to incorporate features from popular magazines. In the 1980s, *Clarín* was the most widely read newspaper in Argentina, although it had not yet reached its peak.

In 1981, Marcelo Pichon-Riviere, son of the famous psychoanalyst Enrique Pichon-Riviere, became the head of the Culture supplement. In addition, intellectuals associated with Peronism, including Jorge Rivera and Aníbal Ford, gained leverage and brought the focus back to the question of a national culture, particularly of an Argentine popular culture. This approach was not new to the newspaper, but it adopted a more celebratory tone of the plebeian and popular than during the previous period. As Roxana Patino (1997) points out,

> The concept of Argentine popular culture is associated, in the first place, with that of regional and indigenous cultures, but far from picturesquism, it comes close to denounce their marginalization. It is also associated with the folkloric aspects of art: popular music and theater, folkloric literature, handicrafts, and finally, urban popular cultures, in a spectrum ranging from *lunfardo* and tango to the analysis of communication media and daily life patterns.

Borges remained a key figure as a central writer for *Clarín* for decades, mirroring his dominant position in the literary field. There were numerous front pages in which, as if in a sort of game of inclusions, Borges talks about other writers: Cortázar, Martínez Estrada, Sarmiento, Wilde, etc. In reality, *Clarín* did not refresh its "literary cast." There was, instead, a continuity from the previous period that repeated the convention of interviewing major writers and talking about their works or having them talk about other authors. For Patino,

> A preference for authors of the 1960s and 1970s is still obvious (Antonio Di Benedetto, Daniel Moyano, Héctor Tizón, Tomás Eloy Martínez, for example), to the detriment of authors of the so-called 'avant-garde,' who had a very weak presence in the supplement, only represented by César Aira.
>
> (1997)

At the end of 1989, *Clarín* took over one of the main TV channels in Buenos Aires[18] (Channel 13) and made official its participation in a radio station that it had controlled through front men. And in 1990, Cytrynblum – who had nurtured a journalistic and cultural approach that was sensitive to the daily life of the middle and popular classes – left his position and was replaced by Roberto Guareschi, who took office with the declared intention of modernizing and professionalizing the newspaper.

There is broad consensus from the people interviewed about the importance of Guareschi. Aulicino points out,

> Guareschi brought with him a more modern orientation, more openness in cultural terms, a position that was more eclectic and much more marked by global journalism. He had a cosmopolitan

vision. He was interested in international politics and the global cultural scene, and he put a lot of emphasis on the area of culture. He underscored the importance of science, technology and ecology. He brought out many more products, more supplements, more additions. *Viva* magazine came out, more comprehensive and more complete.

According to Sivak, he had a global perspective. To improve the newspaper, he drew on successful experiences from elsewhere:

> Guareschi introduced the idea of looking at the cultural supplement of the *New York Times*. He sought journalistic excellence. But keeping the popular. He promoted the use of the word '*gente*' instead of 'Argentinians' or 'society.' But above all, he discontinued the use of the word '*pueblo*.'

And Lavieri notes,

> The newspaper set out to be the best Spanish-language newspaper. Such was Guareschi's project. It was a leader in sales, and they wanted to make it the best. With Guareschi, two changes occurred: he attracted many young people (between 20 and 30 years old), who joined the newspaper to liven up the old editorial staff of *Clarín,* and he brought many journalists from *Gente* magazine to give the newspaper an upbeat tone. These are indicators that the readership was more middle class than upper class.

According to Graciela Mochkofsky (2011), an element that should be taken into account is the emergence of the newspaper *Página 12*, which had been gaining popularity since the late 1980s based on investigative journalism and a new style.

As part of the newspaper's redesign and at the initiative of Guareschi, *Clarín* hired external national and international consultants. Some of them were prominent scholars in the field of communication and semiology. Among the national advisors, Eliseo Verón, Oscar Landi and Aníbal Ford stand out. They carried out analyses, contributed intelligence, reflection and projection to corporate management and provided decisive inputs in this "modernizing" stage. The notion of "multi-target" has its origins in Verón's own discussions and his reading contract with *Clarín*.

The participation of these scholars was more directly aimed at advising the board of directors on how to position the newspaper and conceiving the global strategy, than issuing guidelines for journalistic work. According to sources consulted for this book, this type of input was scarce in the newsroom. In any case, scholars contributed intellectual capital and prestige to the newspaper's modernization process.

These changes in the newspaper had a direct impact on sales. In 1993, a record of 717,000 daily copies on average of *Clarín* were sold during the year, with a peak of 1,230,000 copies on Sundays. Considering that the newspaper had a readership metric of 4, the Sunday edition was read by 5 million people, one of every seven Argentines, for a total population close to 35 million at that time.

By then, the newspaper's readership had extended well beyond the popular and middle classes. As the Group explains, they strive to produce multi-targeted commodities with a special sensitivity toward the middle class. Studies commissioned in the 1990s by the newspaper itself showed that *Clarín*'s readers were divided as follows: 11 percent, sector ABC1 (high/middle high); 39 percent, sector C2 C3 (middle/middle low); 25 percent, D1 (upper low); and 25 percent, D2 (lower low). An executive from Grupo Clarín reported,

> We were aiming more at multi-segment than at the middle class. We had built a significant positioning in all market segments. We had the highest number of absolute readers in all sectors. We had more readers in ABC1 than *La Nación*, and more than *Diario Popular* in the lower sectors. In the middle class, it was the most popular paper in absolute and relative terms.

The 1990s saw the consolidation of *Clarín* as the best-selling and most influential newspaper, but also the rise of the *Clarín* conglomerate. With *Radio Mitre*, it solidified a fully-fledged offering for the middle classes of Buenos Aires. *Mitre* became a leader in audience metrics when *Clarín* took over it in the 1990s, a position it has maintained and from which it was only dislodged by *Radio 10* between 2004 and 2013. *Mitre* has always held a very strong position among the urban middle class in the middle neighborhoods of the Buenos Aires Metropolitan Area.

Nevertheless, Magnetto's great aspiration was to acquire a television channel, which he achieved in 1989 when he won the tender for the privatization of *Canal 13*. In the first years, the television channel would not make the profit that the newspaper made, but it gave the Group a presence in all media segments, which reinforced each other.

However, *Canal 13*'s profile was more aimed at the ABC1 segment. Although all advertising-funded channels must have a generalist and popular orientation, *Canal 13* positioned itself mainly as the option of the highest socioeconomic levels. This is why, although the station was second in audience measurements during most years, in many cases it surpassed its main competitor in sales, since advertising fees were higher due to the segment that watched *Canal 13*.

Another aspect that should be highlighted is that *Canal 13* advocated for broadcasting national fiction. In 1995, it produced a very successful comedy of manners[19] in association with external producers, and since then prime time has featured national fiction. According to Grupo Clarín directors, after the acquisition of the channel, shareholders understood that the key differentiator should be meeting the new demands with national quality content.

The evolution of *Clarín* into a multimedia group with offerings in the three media segments fostered new relationships within the Group. Several journalists who worked at the newspaper pointed out that *Canal 13* had great influence on what was included in the show pages of the *Clarín* newspaper. In fact, they refer to some sort of internal resistance, reluctant as they were to give in to the commercial logic of multimedia. Lavieri points out, "There was no agreement among the brands. There was competition, envy, contempt by the editorial staff towards audiovisual media. There was no obligatory convergence or journalistic coordination."

The expansion into a cross-media group had further consequences. On the one hand, the diversification in written press option. For example, the launch of the sports newspaper *Olé* stands out. Designed for an audience of soccer fans (with soccer as a passion for most Argentines), its journalistic agenda was not lacking in chauvinism and machismo. While it can be inferred that these were aspects that were (and still are) present in the soccer environment, *Clarín*'s offering took up several of its most controversial aspects to ensure success. As Aulicino points out, "*Olé* strove to reach soccer fans. They went in search of another audience, different from the traditional *Clarín* audience."

The passion for soccer is also related to another of the Group's ventures that had a much broader focus. Throughout the 1990s, *Clarín* invested in cable television and in order to build customer loyalty, one of its usual resources was the exclusive offer of encrypted soccer. Because of this, it was accused of anti-competitive practices by several smaller cable companies. Beyond soccer, cable television gave the Group two significant opportunities. First, to have a national offer, a direct connection to the whole Argentine citizenship. Although *Clarín*'s products were consumed throughout the country, its production was Buenos Aires-based, while with cable television the sale of connections was at the local level. Second, and perhaps more importantly, with cable TV the Group entered directly into the home, with a strategy to offer services rather than information products. This is an important precedent for a new business concept, where media loses importance as the main generator of income. This is not a minor issue for a company such as *Clarín* that is oriented to the search for profitability.

Within their cable programming, Grupo Clarín's corporate brands led the news segment and included channels that showed reruns of old television hits and national cinema that drew a larger audience than expected. Although material from Hollywood predominated in the whole programming grid due to a cost issue, the emblematic content of *Clarín* was sports, news and the revitalization of national culture. In other words, it reproduced important traits that were present in the logic with which the newspaper was built.

But these changes within the structure of the Group had an impact on the contents of the paper and cultural topics were given renewed attention during Guareschi's management. In 1991, the supplement called "Second Section" was launched, featuring current political and cultural debates. This section was a response to the challenge set by the recently launched newspaper *Página 12* and, with that competition in mind, the supplement featured op-ed pieces, subjects of intellectual debate, but lighter in tone than those included in the cultural section. In 1998, Second Section was dissolved and the supplement *Zona*, with a center-left orientation, was added to the newspaper. In this supplement, there was broad participation by intellectuals who later became supporters of Kirchnerism and who would enter into an open confrontation with *Clarín* ten years later. At the same time, as Sivak points out, "Culture and Nation set out to lessen the solemnity of the supplement and new content was added to literature, such as anthropology, daily life and mass culture studies" (2015: 207). The Group's readership reports indicated that only 10 percent of *Clarín*'s buyers were interested in the cultural supplement.

With the expansion and diversification of its offer, the newspaper sought to remain the paper of choice for the majority of Argentines, something it achieved over the decade of the 1990s. Aulicino notes that it was a newspaper with a segment orientation.

> It was for all, because it had something for everyone, sections for each reader. Everyone found what they wanted. From the most refined to the most populist. It was designed with the segmentation of readers in mind and there was a supplement for each segment. There were sections in which the analytical thinking took

precedence and others that were marked by a populist or sensationalist rhetoric, although in a lesser degree than in earlier years. The idea was that everyone could read it. It was neither decidedly populist – like the popular newspapers – nor was it serious enough to be included among the main newspapers.

However, the newspaper continued to reflect the sensibility of the middle class. It was anchored in the daily culture of Argentines and especially *porteños*.[20] With Guareschi, the simple formula of the Cytrynblum era became more complex. There was growing diversity in the content supply, with a new model that combined the popular and the serious. As opposed to the traditional angle on culture which focused on the national culture, Guareschi interests broadened toward the globalized world. Complexity was thought to contribute to a better and more diverse newspaper, but without affecting sales. The newspaper knew how to strike a balance so as to retain its popular readership while engaging readers in the upper middle sectors. Aulicino points out that

> it was offensive for *Clarín* not be considered a serious newspaper. The idea was to make a culturally complex newspaper, by virtue of its scope. It was intended to be read by everyone, without being vulgar or populist. The same was true for its cultural approach. The orientation the newspaper officially had was the same for all its production: a national and popular orientation, and at times much more popular than national.

It should be noted that during the 1990s, there had been a significant inflow of foreign capital investment into the communications sector. But Clarín took advantage of its status as a national Group to appear close to the audience. Nevertheless, the formation of an increasingly powerful cross-media group, both economically and symbolically, also created a list of adversaries.

At the end of the 1990s, the conglomerate's overall level of indebtedness led it to accept the entry of foreign capital into the Corporate Group. Although this did not imply changes in its cultural offer, the logic of profit now prevailed over any other criterion. The 1990s was the decade of great development for Clarín, both in its undisputed hegemony in the print market and for its impressive expansion in audiovisual media, especially in free-to-air and pay television.

2001–2009: Recovery and National Culture

In December 2001, Argentina faced an acute crisis that began as an economic crisis but rapidly expanded into the political and social spheres. Grupo Clarín was heavily affected by the situation. First, because of its hefty debt in dollars (the exit from the crisis implied a strong depreciation of the Argentine currency), and, second, because all of its products were intended for the domestic market. Also, there was a significant fall in consumption in middle- and low-income households, and cultural goods usually showed a fairly elastic demand. In those difficult years, Grupo Clarín accentuated its Argentine profile: it promoted *truco*[21] championships, local cooking courses and a set of references linked to what it understood as the "true Argentine character."

The Group was one of the sponsors of the Law for the Preservation of Cultural Assets (*Ley de Preservación de Bienes Culturales*) that exempted cultural industries from the Bankruptcy Law, which permitted creditors to acquire a company's assets to settle its debt. As part of its lobbying strategy, all of the brands in the Group conducted major public campaigns highlighting the importance of maintaining ownership of cultural enterprises in the hands of Argentine capital, given the existing risk of foreignization. The campaign concealed, of course, that the Group's debt levels were much higher than those of other cultural companies, and that this was a result of the need for financing the concentration process it had experienced in the previous decade. Magnetto (2016) alleges that Clarín did not use the aforementioned law, which is as true as the fact that it was not necessary to use it. The mere existence of the law limited the possibilities of external creditors. It functioned as pre-insurance and as a strong bargaining chip.

Unlike the 1990s, during the first years of the 21st century Grupo Clarín had to slow down its expansion plans while it restructured its debt. Only around 2007 did it fulfill an old dream and buy its main competitor in the pay television scene. Thus, the Group became the main pay TV operator in Latin America by number of subscribers.

Within this context of restrictions, one of the most important launches was a cultural magazine called Ñ. With its appearance, the cultural supplements of the newspaper ceased to exist, and culture was assigned only one page in the newspaper, reporting on day-to-day cultural policy.

The launch of Ñ was the result of several market studies indicating that only a minority of *Clarín* readers were interested in serious cultural debate. Since the company found that cultural supplements had a high production cost and low consumption, they were removed from the newspaper and a specialized magazine was launched, which was to be purchased separately from the paper. From then on, access to cultural debates had an additional cost for readers. The underlying idea was that people interested in culture were willing to pay that price. At the head of this project was the new editorial secretary general, Ricardo Kirschbaum. Aulicino gives an account of this process:

> Market studies were key to the appearance of $\tilde{N}$ magazine, which replaced Culture and Nation, published on Thursdays. A survey was conducted which revealed that only ten percent of Clarín's readers were interested in Culture and Nation. The newspaper realized that the money invested was not compensated by the publicity generated by culture. The supplement did not pay off. So, they came up with the idea of the magazine. It was the first optional supplement released by the newspaper. When it came out, it was an absolute novelty and it cost 50 cents.[22] Readers who were interested in it were going to pay that price because it was little money. It was a little less than buying another newspaper. It wasn't too expensive for the type of magazine it was. This decision was made like that. It was a marketing decision, an economic decision. They considered that even if they sold it for that price, the supplement wouldn't recover its costs. And indeed, it didn't compensate for them.

The launch of $\tilde{N}$ can be seen from two different perspectives. The most critical voices argue that this movement deepened a process of commoditization of the entire range of Grupo Clarín's journalistic products, which expanded even into the area of culture. Others found that the decision produced a quality cultural magazine by mitigating the losses generated by the newspaper supplement. The newspaper's directors have stated that it was necessary to make a quality product at a reasonable price and to maintain sustainability. For their part, several *Clarín* journalists wondered about the point of producing a million cultural supplements when their readership did not exceed 100,000 people.

Conceived as a weekly magazine, $\tilde{N}$ had 48 pages intended to cover a wide range of topics pertaining to culture, from literary reviews to national and global philosophical and sociological debates. Once a month, it presented special dossiers that increased the number of pages.

To answer the question, What is culture for *Ñ*?, Juan Bedoian, its first director, in issue #212 of *Ñ* magazine wrote, "We understand culture not only as the conforming spirit that dictates the styles and forms of intellectual work, but as an organizing principle of experience, the feeling of a community." According to this text, *Ñ* proposed to transcend the identification between culture and intellectual creation, to understand culture as a construction of meaning that encompasses the whole experience (Dillon, 2011). For Flavia Costa,[23]

> Between 1997 and 2007, the idea of the Culture supplement and then *Ñ* was quite homogeneous because it was linked to what we would classically refer to as 'high culture,' i.e., culture understood in a restricted way. Not in an anthropological sense. Themes were basically literature, the world of cinema, the classics of film, theatrical dramaturgy – more than the theatrical show. The cultural themes of the essayist type, philosophical themes, contemporary thought, and also part of the cultural debates of the moment or the cultural perspective of the political debate of the moment did also find their place there. In this respect, the influence of Josefina Ludmer is easily traced. She encouraged us to politicize the supplement in that sense. To give a significant place to political philosophy and the political perspective of the contemporary.

When presenting the first number, the Secretary General of *Clarín*, Ricardo Kirschbaum, pointed out, "The modern cultural magazine *Ñ* tries to translate, with an ample view, all the manifestations of culture – in its widest sense – with depth and clarity." He later added, "Argentine culture is progress, stimulus, pride and resistance. For that space, we have created *Ñ* and its paradigm serves as a way to hold on to an idea of a country affected by recurrent crises." The launch of *Ñ* allowed *Clarín* to reconcile its logic of profitable economic enterprise with a discourse of modernity, diversity and defense of Argentine culture. As previously noted, *Ñ* emerged in a context in which the Group sought to revalue the Latin and the Argentine. The use of the letter *Ñ* also implies the vindication of the particularity of the Spanish language.

In its early stages, and at least during its first three years, *Ñ* became a sales success with a print run of around 80,000 copies per week. But it reached peaks of more than 100,000 and sold 120,000 the day that the most famous tango singer, Carlos Gardel, was featured on the cover of the magazine, in June 2005, on the 70th anniversary of his death. Few Argentine newspapers of the time sold that many copies.

According to Aulicino, a big advantage was that the writing staff of Ñ was very diverse, giving rise to a plurality of approaches: "It was like a summary of all you had to know about culture." He also points out that although political pressures were much less acute than in other sections, the emphasis from management was on the need to find an average reader in the sense of the majority reader. For example, "the choice of the central theme for the cover was made on the basis of how many people could be interested in the topic." In this sense, he recalls that the most sought-after covers were those linked to characters of the Argentine popular culture, such as the aforementioned case of Gardel or the comic book author Roberto Fontanarrosa: "Because Fontanarrosa was the average". In its diversity, Ñ gave space to positions that have traditionally been called "leftist" or "progressive."

Flavia Costa, on the other hand, has other thoughts about the diversity of readers who thought from Ñ:

> "We were writing for an audience that, without being a subject-matter expert, was interested in the topic. In general, all readers interested in a topic were considered, whether they were experts or not. So, if the reader was an expert, the journalist had to offer them a piece of information that they did not have, and offer the non-expert a clear explanation of the topic, an overview. Journalists knew that the specific piece of information that was intended for the expert may not be completely grasped by non-experts, who might miss it entirely, but that was not a problem. We were very clear that our readers were very different people from very different parts of the country who wanted to have specific information on the cultural field in a restricted sense. We struggled with the occasional demand to popularize the supplement."

The magazine faced the complex task of reaching a wide readership while focusing on very specific content. In a study that analyzes in detail the first years of Ñ magazine, Alfredo Dillon (2011) highlights that it is more like a literary magazine than *Clarín*'s traditional supplements (such as Culture and Nation). This is also stressed by Héctor Pavón, who notes that the emergence of Ñ was contemporaneous with the decline of cultural magazines that had sprung up during the dictatorship, had stayed afloat during the democratic transition, weakened toward the end of Menemism and finally disappeared with the economic crisis of 2001.

Dillon's study of the early years of Ñ confirms the thematic diversity of the journal. He notes that special attention was given to the art market, and sociological and anthropological debates also found their place. For Dillon, "Ñ proposes a more attentive look at social processes." According to him, the magazine strikes a balance between national and international contents, with a slight prevalence of the former. Sharp imbalance does exist, however, within the national content, marked by a strong focus on the City of Buenos Aires, with the rest of the country playing a minor role. This entailed a contradiction for the editorial staff. Aulicino states that more than half of the copies of Ñ were sold in the provinces. For his part, Pavón relates various attempts by the editorial staff to report on the artistic and intellectual debates with a federal approach, although in the end the coverage was limited to Buenos Aires, and, to a much lesser extent, to Rosario, Córdoba and Mendoza. Regardless of intentions, the cultural industry is based in Buenos Aires. From a critical perspective, Oropeza (2011) points out,

> In line with this restoration movement, the names of national culture can be found flipping through the issues of the magazine, repeated to the point of paroxysm. In the manner of a gallery of geniuses, established writers are the common currency in which the traditional Argentine cultural canon is reaffirmed. Besides, this legitimate tour mirrors to a high degree the tastes and tendencies of Buenos Aires city and its surroundings. A clear example is that the events included in the weekly agenda are almost exclusively from the capital city or at most the province of Buenos Aires.

From its beginnings, the magazine has maintained a fruitful relationship with the intellectual field. In a tacit agreement of mutual convenience, it was nourished by the ideas of many of the most outstanding thinkers who in return received public visibility that would have been very difficult for them to achieve in the university and intellectual spheres. Unlike the culture pages of a newspaper, the magazine had to be paid for, and therefore it was assumed the reader had some concrete interest in cultural debates. It segmented the public, while at the same time, brought it closer together. Aulicino points out that the intellectual world actively participated in Ñ. Pavón recalls having consulted key sources about their relationship with the magazine, and the response was that there were always two or three interesting stories. The magazine was read. From the other side, González recognizes that although he had to adjust his style minimally when he wrote in Ñ, the magazine was an important cultural reference. For González,

Ñ became a beacon of culture in Argentina, which helped promote young writers.

The editing of Ñ was not without debates between those who sought the most popular approach to intellectual debate and those who sought to account for the complexity of the problem. This tension gradually gave way. After years of splendor, in 2007 the magazine's circulation began to decline and dropped to 30,000 copies by the end of the first decade of the 21st century. A report by the Circulation Verification Institute (*Instituto Verificador de Circulaciones*) in July 2019 shows that the circulation of the magazine had fallen to 8,200 copies. As we will see in the next section, digitization reconfigured the consumption of cultural products.

Ñ magazine is representative of the evolution of the cultural profile of Grupo Clarín. Its origin was in the search for profitability, and to that end it had to be transformed into a mass product for which audiences were willing to pay. It has been aimed, above all, at the middle sectors, although at the same time it does not rule out wider audiences, in this case mainly in the cultural field. With a very critical perspective, Oropeza asserts that the magazine is shaped to

> the taste of the middle sectors of society that prefer the avant-garde once it has the stamp of official approval, that is, when it is no longer avant-garde, and it disseminates artistic expressions that are deprived of their creative power and conform to outmoded and outdated aesthetic conventions.

In other words, Ñ magazine appears as a theme park of obsolete cultural material hidden under a "right-thinking" patina. Finally, the magazine is presented as an affirmation of Argentine culture, but at the same time tries to establish dialogue with global modernity. The Group that aspired to totality created a cultural magazine with that same intention. As Pavón explains: "In 2003, we wanted to do everything. To have the best writers, the best debates, to give an account of the cinema, the theater, the art world."

2009–2020: Confrontation and Metamorphosis

Considered from an economic angle, perhaps what happened from 2009 onward should not be separated from the previous stage. Two facts, or unrelated issues that coincide in time, are important to analyze the cultural dynamics of Grupo Clarín from the second decade of the 21st century.

On the one hand, the confrontation of Grupo Clarín with Cristina Fernández de Kirchner's administrations led *Clarín* to "war journalism," according to one of the newspaper's chief editors. We will try to analyze the effects of this situation on the cultural profile of the Group.

Second, and more permanently, is the impact of digitization on the media offer. The changes in media consumption are something that both managers and editors are concerned about, although the word most often used is "uncertainty." The analog world at least had its certainties, which vanished like everything else that is solid.

Previous chapters have mentioned the confrontation between Grupo Clarín and the two administrations of Cristina Fernández de Kirchner (2007–2015). One of the effects at the level of content is that the political dispute homogenized the profile of Grupo Clarín's media. While until 2009, as noted by Sivak (2015), the newspaper was more open to dialogue than other media products, since the sanctioning of the Audiovisual Communication Services Law (*Ley de Servicios de Comunicación Audiovisual*) all content was the outcome of a clear and strong editorial line: To oppose Kirchnerism.

While Kirchnerism responded from the media outlets it controlled by deepening the semiotic analysis of the opposition media discourse, the condensation of Clarín's editorial line had an effect on the Group's audiences. While on previous occasions the changes in the editorial line (for example, the change from Peronism to anti-Peronism in 1955) had no influence, on this occasion the middle-class sectors who supported Cristina Fernández de Kirchner reduced their consumption of Grupo Clarín's media. In this sense, Sivak claims:

> Now the Kirchnerist reader is excluded. Never before had there been a decision to exclude such an important group of readers. The shift from Peronist to Anti-Peronist in 1955 did not have any cost in terms of readers. Consumers did not care about the change in line. That reader of *Clarín* was not so attentive to the editorial line. They were not too interested in politics. Until the conflict with Kirchnerism, *Clarín*'s readers were not required to have any political commitment.

This situation must also be understood in the context of an overall decrease in media consumption due to the effects of digitization. As Pavón states: "It coincides with a certain technological development that changes the agenda, or broadens it, and that also changes supports and languages. Now it is more complicated." In this sense, the consumption of media linked to political identities needs to be studied in depth. In any case, the growth in consumption of a pay TV subscription channel (*C5N*) with a clear Kirchnerist orientation gives a clue to some of the changes that were taking place. For the first time in decades, the news channel of Grupo Clarín (*TN*) was displaced from first place in the pay TV ratings.

At the same time, the content itself was mutating. In the cultural field, the intellectuals linked to Kirchnerism gradually reduced their presence. Both the editors of the newspaper and the intellectuals themselves admit they had lost interest in each other. While *Clarín's* cultural segment had previously shown an interesting intellectual diversity, after 2010 it gave all its attention to intellectuals critical of Kirchnerism.

On the other hand, digitization has implied a fundamental change for media markets because it put an end to the certainties of the analog business model in which *Clarín* had been a clear primus inter pares in the Argentine market. However, Magnetto himself notes:

> Nobody knows for sure how our market will be reconfigured, and we all wonder if professional journalistic organizations will remain where they are. If the traditional media – let's call it that – will be profitable to produce quality content, if they will be able to finance themselves with online advertising, what space cable TV will have in the convergence market and so many questions like that. I think that, faced with uncertainty, two different approaches can be applied simultaneously. Neither of them guarantees results, because guaranteed results are just not possible nowadays. However, we believe that we are moving in the direction set by technological, production and consumption trends. As far as the corporate strategy is concerned, we must have the intelligence and capacity to take strategic steps to not lose prestige and significance in the market, to not increase our vulnerability and avoid dissolution when facing the phenomenon of convergence. The investments we are making to strengthen our distribution network and the incorporation of mobility go in that direction.
>
> (2016: 235)

The Group's strategy was to replace the media as a source of income. As seen in Chapter 3, the main income of Grupo Clarín from 2007 onward was from the provision of connectivity services, first for cable television and internet access, and from 2018 for mobile telephony.

And this led to rethinking the place of the media, an issue of concern for Magnetto:

> In the world of content, we have to continue deepening the transformations that audiences and technological changes are demanding from us. Here our success will depend, to a great extent, on what we can do to maintain our journalistic role in a much more multipolar universe, with social networks as central actors, with new references constantly emerging, with audiences that legitimize or delegitimize the discourse of the media. We live in a universe where no institution has hegemony over public conversation and where, in order to stand out, we have to exert our creativity. It is as important to generate quality content as it is to develop the tools to reach those who need to consume it in the right moment and with the right format and device. We all learn from each other.
> (2016: 235)

Of course, up until the current moment, the digital content part, although it can be considered successful in quantitative terms, has failed to generate benefits for the Group. As Sivak points out, Magnetto has always acted more as an industrial entrepreneur than as a technological innovator (2015: 392).

The changes and challenge of digitization have also been felt by the editorial staff. Accustomed to the previously massive physical scale, they have had to reinvent themselves in a context where the search for massive scale subordinates the editorial line to the rationale of click-through ratios. This has had an impact on cultural products, which are finding it increasingly difficult to be part of *Clarín*. To access Ñ magazine, for example, it is necessary to double-click on a side bar of the home page. First, readers must access "Culture" and from there they are redirected to Ñ. As Pavón points out:

> One consequence of all this is how hard it is to be on *Clarín's* home page. We don't get to interest the generation that is working on Clarín.com, which is the landing page, and it's like talking to a call center employee. We have a sub-home. It's a vertical. We have to go to Culture. Two clicks. It's very difficult to convince people working on the home page of the importance of a Culture story. We are all acquiring the skills of writing good headlines. Now we have to stir up intrigue but without falling into sensationalism. They ask you to provide stories such as 'the seven books you should read this summer.'

That is why for some journalists the digital transformation is more important than the fight against Kirchnerism. Especially because it has practical effects on their own working conditions: The workforce has been reduced. Today Ñ is produced by 5 journalists, while before there were 25. If income drops, expenses must be cut. In other words, it is a company that produces cultural content, but is guided by economic criteria.

Culture for All

There is a substantive body of academic and journalistic studies on Grupo Clarín. Its economic structure and political influence have been studied and some of its contents dissected. However, there are not many studies that address *Clarín's* cultural conception. This is noteworthy, considering that the company's main products are cultural goods. Looking back on the relationship between *Clarín* and culture, it can be seen that the cultural project was subordinated to the company's two backbones: politics and economics. While the newspaper was created to promote the political figure of Noble and went through a second stage that contributed to the dissemination of Developmentalist ideas, since the early 1980s Grupo Clarín has been organized around the search for profit and growth. From the first moment, when it was marked by a superstructural and eminently ideological rationale, it transitioned into a company guided by the structural needs of economic development. In the transition from politics to economic pragmatism, culture was downgraded to a less relevant place.

Clarín's cultural profile has changed over the years. However, some continuities can be observed, especially the idea of seeking a wide audience. Unlike some of its competitors, *Clarín* does not fragment or exclude. It aspires to encompass everyone as part of its audience, because ultimately its audience is the source of its income. At the same time, that all-encompassing audience is achieved by taking care of the formal aspects, and trying to avoid sensationalism (with some exceptions, such as *Diario Olé*). Stories are aimed at the middle classes, but also at the popular classes, without excluding the enlightened sectors. As has been pointed out above, a newspaper for all, and culture for all. Costa links the wide-ranging audience with the importance that the middle and popular classes attach to mobility: "Cultural advancement is the substitute for economic advancement. For the middle and lower classes, culture was a very important aspect. It was not a minor thing to be frowned upon. We have a great appreciation for cultural mobility."

Totality has also been expressed in the need to include global perspectives and problems. If the Group opened up to the world through its economic relations, it also did so in its cultural project. Without abandoning the nationalist approach to culture, more and more global intellectual debates have been given attention, with a focus on places that have always dazzled various social classes in Argentina, for instance, New York and Paris.

In the first decades, the renewed commitment of the middle and popular classes to *Clarín*'s products was the object of desire of those who wanted to have political influence. For others, it was the source of significant income. In the last decade, Grupo Clarín has had to face a double challenge: the difficulty of sustaining its massive scale in the digital environment, while becoming a provider of telecommunications services, thus relegating communication and culture to a secondary position.

Clarín has represented moderate cultural nationalism and was broad-minded enough to attract the masses – a construction of national culture with a *porteño* accent to contribute to hegemony, first political, and, later on, economic.

Notes

1 *Crítica* was a newspaper that appeared in 1913. It had an unprecedented style for the time, with big headlines on the title page and plenty of illustrations, as well as extensive use of slang.
2 Juan Perón was elected in February 1946 for a first term (1946–1952) and reelected in November 1951 for a second term (1952–1958). In September 1955, he was overthrown by a military coup.
3 Telephone interview.
4 Telephone interview.
5 In 1962, the government of Arturo Frondizi was overthrown by a new military coup.
6 Telephone conversation.
7 This is the name by which the political alliance between Frondizi and Frigerio is known. They created a political party (*Movimiento de Integración y Desarrollo*) through which they tried to influence Argentine politics for decades, with varying degrees of success.
8 Telephone interview.
9 Father of the rock musicians Andrés and Javier, well known in Latin America and Spain.
10 Among the missing *Clarín* journalists are Enrique Raab, Luis Guagnini, Paco Urondo, Ernesto Fossat and Edgardo Sajón.
11 Telephone interview.
12 In-person interview.
13 In-person interview.
14 Telephone interview.

15 Telephone interview.
16 Personal correspondence.
17 Telephone interview.
18 The Argentine TV system has one particularity: There are no nationwide TV licenses except for the state-run channel. However, due to a series of business or ownership relations, the programming of Buenos Aires city channels is redistributed throughout the country.
19 The show was called *Poliladron* and was produced by Polka, led by actor and entrepreneur Adrian Suar. That production company was later sold to Grupo Clarín and Suar was appointed content manager for *Canal 13*.
20 *Porteños:* From the port. This is how Buenos Aires City inhabitants are referred to throughout the country.
21 The most popular card game in the country.
22 At that time, the equivalent of US$ 50 cents.
23 Telephone interview.

References

Bayer, Osvaldo (2003). "Prólogo: Introducción con nostalgias, flores y heridas", in P. Llonto *La Noble Ernestina* (pp. 11–17). Buenos Aires: Astralib.

Dillon, Alfredo (2011). *La construcción periodística del campo cultural*. Buenos Aires: Educa.

Frigerio, Rogelio (1968). *Integración Regional instrumento del monopolio*. Buenos Aires: Editorial Hernández.

Frigerio, Rogelio (1976). *Conferencia sobre Cultura Nacional*. Buenos Aires: Crisol.

Hora, Roy (2020). "17 de octubre: la promesa, la apuesta y la lealtad", in *La Vanguardia Digital*, recuperado de. http://www.lavanguardiadigital.com.ar/index.php/2020/10/17/17-de-octubre-la-promesa-la-apuesta-y-la-lealtad/

López, José (2008). *El hombre de Clarín. Vida pública y privada de Héctor Magnetto*. Buenos Aires: Sudamericana.

Magnetto, Héctor (2016). *Así lo viví. El poder, los medios y la política en Argentina*. Buenos Aires: Planeta.

Mochkofsky, Graciela (2011). *Pecado original. Clarín, los Kirchner y la lucha por el poder*. Buenos Aires: Planeta.

Oropeza, Mariano (2011). "Había una vez más ... La cultura argentina en la revista cultural Ñ", en L. Otrocki y C. Giordano (eds.). *Cuestiones sobre medios masivos e industrias culturales: análisis de mensajes, textos, discursos y narrativas*. La Plata: Universidad Nacional de La Plata. https://www.google.com/search?client=firefox-b-d&q=HAB%C3%8DA+UNA+VEZ+M%C3%81S...+LA+CULTURA+ARGENTINA+EN+LAREVISTA+CULTURAL+%C3%91Mariano+OropezaUniversidad+de+Buenos+Aires

Patiño, Roxana (1997). "Democratizar/ modernizar: los suplementos culturales en la transición argentina". *Revista Hispamérica*, 26(78), 3–16.

Rivera, Jorge (1995). *El periodismo cultural*. Buenos Aires: Paidós.

Sivak, Martín (2013). *Clarín. Una historia.* Buenos Aires: Planeta.
Sivak, Martín (2015). *Clarín. La era Magnetto.* Buenos Aires: Planeta.

Interviews

Blanca Rébori. Journalist, *Clarín*, 1967–1976. Co-founder of Culture and Nation Supplement. September 23, 2020.
Albino Gómez. Director, Culture and Nation Supplement, 1975–1976. September 23, 2020.
Omar Lavieri. Journalist, *Clarín*, 1991–1998 and 2009–2013. October 1, 2020.
Martín Sivak. Journalist. October 2, 2020.
Jorge Aulicino. Journalist / Editor of Cultural Supplement and *Ñ* magazine, 1980–1988 and 1992–2012. October 7, 2020.
Horacio González. Essayist and Cultural Critic. October 9, 2020.
Guillermo Ariza. Director, Culture and Nation Supplement, 1977–1981. October 13, 2020.
Héctor Pavón. Editor of *Ñ* magazine, 2003–2020. October 17, 2020.
Flavia Costa. Writer, *Ñ* magazine, 1997–2007. October 28, 2020.

Conclusion

Governments Have Passed. Clarín Has Stayed. What Might Its Future Look Like?

Grupo Clarín is a truly successful business group from an economic perspective. Considering the political and economic spasms Argentina experienced over the 75 years of the conglomerate's existence, this is indicative of the ability and talent of its successive corporate management teams to deal with – and take advantage of – recent storms in national contemporary history. Furthermore, Grupo Clarín is interesting for a number of other reasons: The versatility of its political relations with different civil and military governments, both constitutional and dictatorial regimes; its economic progress and consolidation, first as a multimedia group and then as an integrated telecom, ICT and media conglomerate at the national level with barely any international projection; and as a multi-class cultural driver for decades, as well as an intellectual mainstay and representative of the middle-class sectors.

But throughout its history, Grupo Clarín has shown many dark spots in several cases coinciding with the most critical periods of contemporary Argentine history. Would it be acceptable for leading journalistic companies around the world to become partners of the state in the production of the industry's critical content, with preferential treatment vis-à-vis their competitors? Moreover, would such a partnership with the state be acceptable, given that it sprung from a dictatorship responsible for crimes against humanity?

Grupo Clarín's participation in forums and press associations at the continental and world level, as well as intense public relations activity in recent decades and prizes won in various categories, could indicate that mainstream media in developed countries may be willing to accept certain behaviors in peripheral countries that would not be admissible in their own nations. Perhaps there is minimal understanding of large media groups residing outside the epicenter of capitalism due to the relatively limited knowledge of their history and performance. Hence, the relevance of this study as part of research by colleagues from different latitudes, designed to shed light on media and information-communication groups beyond the borders of First World nations.

The history of Grupo Clarín is noticeable for its chiaroscuros. Unlike *Folha de Sao Paulo*, for instance, Grupo Clarín has never been self-critical of its explicit support for all coups d'état and, in particular, for the last dictatorship in Argentina. Considering such a background, is Grupo Clarín in a position to uphold a discourse of respect for democratic institutions? After all, its top managers today are the same as in the past.

Furthermore, the history of Grupo Clarín has been marked by two personalities: Roberto Noble and Hector Magnetto. During the very short period during which neither of them was running the company (1969 to 1972), the newspaper almost disappeared. Indeed, from the death of Noble in 1969 until the 1972 entry of Magnetto and his associates, as well as accountants Hector Aranda and Lucio Pagliaro (current shareholders of the Group, but with smaller stakes than Magnetto), the economic disorders of the company intensified. During that period, the company lacked a captain capable of setting the right course for the vessel, until Magnetto arrived and set accounts in order. His measures also had repercussions on the newsroom, which experienced its first massive layoffs in the turbulent early years of the 1970s.

It is also notable that during the Group's history which stretches over more than seven decades, it has never had significant shareholder dispersion. Such stability is in contrast to the shareholding changes that are typical of news companies in developed countries. However, it is not a rare arrangement in Latin America: The cases of the Mexican Grupo Televisa or the Brazilian Grupo Globo also show continuities within the family tradition of an integrated shareholding structure. On the other hand, Grupo Clarín, unlike the large conglomerates of Mexico and Brazil, built its shareholding homogeneity based on the notion of the "extended family." Magnetto and his descendants are not part of the Noble lineage; Marcela and Felipe Noble Herrera also were not related to the founder of the newspaper, but were adopted in an irregular process by his widow. Other main shareholders, including Aranda, Pagliaro and their children, are part of Magnetto's entourage with no family ties to Noble.

128 Conclusion

Shareholding stability and cohesion have provided consistency to the core of Grupo Clarín owners and leaders, but, at the same time, held back capital expansion to other productive activities, restrained capital circulation and business with third parties when the Group has not been at the helm of operations and, in the opinion of the authors, have resulted in limited and unsuccessful internationalization. Another reason for this is that the Argentine market is relatively small compared to Mexico or Brazil, where highly concentrated multimedia groups have not succeeded–as Clarín did– in dominating the telecommunications segment, but due to the scale of their respective economies, achieved much higher business volumes, including their expansion abroad. Conversely, unlike other groups, such as Cisneros (Venezuela) and Santo Domingo (Colombia), whose parent companies operate in economies resembling Argentina, Grupo Clarín did not rally the diversified support that those conglomerates had for their media units. In recent years, Grupo Clarín unleashed a gigantic cash flow – relative to the economics of its powerful media group – with the Cablevisión-Telecom merger, which was carried out thanks to the policies of former president Mauricio Macri.

Even considering historical differences that set them apart, and despite not having been contemporaneous in the organization, Noble and Magnetto displayed similar skills: They were both good at building close ties with governments beyond ideologies. Furthermore, both men developed aggressive and winning strategies to seize opportunities in the media landscape afforded by Argentina's political and economic shifts in their respective tenures. Magnetto had an additional strength: A strategic understanding of the transformations of the infotainment sector that Noble did not need to deploy because, on the one hand, technology transformations were less pronounced between the 1940s and 1960s and, on the other hand, the newspaper was weaker in relative terms during its first 25 years of existence. Noble's interest in the supply of printing paper, however, is an indication that he understood how to articulate the value chain of the industry.

Though playing his part in a different era, Magnetto was no stranger to the mutation of journalism, a trade that evolved from the bohemian, lavish, leftist principles and vast erudite culture typical of Noble's time, toward the delivery of valuable information for corporate growth, mainly guided by placing high stakes on economic expansion.

The stages in Grupo Clarín's evolution under the leadership of Noble and Magnetto (with the interregnum of Frigerio's tenure) point to the advantages that a personal approach brings in terms of execution efficiency and speedy decision-making. But they also underscore the limitations of leaders who surrounded themselves with aides who neither questioned nor challenged the decisions or the vertical power scheme, coupled with the limitations of a project that is exclusively dependent on the decisions of a single leader.

The executive and strategic vision of the Group's leadership is evident in the expansive concentration during the shaping of Grupo Clarín as a multimedia group; the subsequent defensive concentration requiring laborious lobbying to protect itself against claims from external creditors following the debacle of the Argentine economy in late 2001 and the downfall of the peso-dollar convertibility; and the negotiations first with Kirchner and then with Macri to achieve the mergers of Multicanal and Cablevisión in 2007, and Cablevisión and Telecom in 2017 and 2018. This can be contrasted with a decision-making style that is more reliant on negotiations between partners and executives, as deployed by other smaller national groups (Vila-Manzano, Indalo), as well as by foreign groups (Claro, Telefónica, Viacom) that are active in some of the segments where Grupo Clarín operates.

For decades, *Clarín* was very skillful at positioning itself as a multi-class newspaper with an extensive readership, and creating a feeling of belonging in all sectors. Although the Group's audiovisual media outlets connected more with the urban middle classes, they also crossed class borders and bridged ideological divides until the war against Kirchnerism. In 2008, this conflict started to expel audiences and readers that Grupo Clarín had harvested in the equally multi-class ranks of Peronism, in particular, from its most intense and dynamic core over the two previous decades. Thus, the framing of the news and opinions in Grupo Clarín's journalistic products became more and more ideologically homogeneous, and no longer represented the claim of a generalist and all-encompassing view of the entire social, political and ideological spectrum that was analyzed and criticized by Eliseo Verón, the influential advisor to the leadership of Grupo Clarín in the 1990s. The notion of "war journalism" (as the former editor-in-chief Julio Blanck described *Clarín*'s editorial position against the Cristina Fernández de Kirchner administration) has great explanatory power. It summarizes a key transition from a more aseptic conception of the cleavages caused by the current situation toward taking on the voice of polarized sectors of political identity in Argentina– anti-Kirchnerism and other political sectors associated with Peronism. This has also permeated the "soft zone" of entertainment content, including audiovisual fiction and variety programs, which once flaunted an alleged "a political view" and have now joined the attacks against Kirchnerism.

130 Conclusion

The management of the editorial line of Grupo Clarín's brands faces the challenge of maintaining its appeal to mass audiences typical of the middle segments in a country in which most inhabitants perceive themselves as "middle class" – despite statistics pointing to a generalized impoverishment of the population – while attacking on a daily basis one of the political identities that embodies some of those very sectors of society. These efforts are more effective when amplifying the daily annoyances of the mood of society, which, in regional terms, expresses its claims and protests in a fairly public way, rather than when drawing up an agenda for improvement, or presenting an alternative to political-electoral expressions that also represent that state of consciousness and organization of Argentinians. Today the editorial line followed by the Group's numerous companies causes no surprise, with all editors, opinion-makers and columnists and most sources subscribing to it. This is possible because, over the last 20 years, the business model and income structure of Grupo Clarín ceased to be dependent on seducing and eliciting the loyalty of diverse audiences, but rather relies on the connectivity and telecommunications segments. The corporate expansion to these markets was catapulted by the previous massiveness and influence of the media, and the political exploitation of these attributes by the Group's leadership. Since then, content has been subordinated to business, just the opposite of what happened before the turn of the millennium.

In its first decades, Grupo Clarín created an identity that became camouflaged with the culture of the middle and popular classes for which it designed appropriate products and offerings. But in the last 20 years, its reconversion as a fixed and mobile telecom carrier added to its difficulty in sustaining its massive impact in digital environments, relegated the Group's production of journalistic content and variety and impacted investments in new formats and products that meet the information, entertainment and education needs of the audience.

Clarín's talent in building a business strategy that started with a newspaper that evolved into an emporium that is increasingly diversified and one of largest employers of Argentina did not translate into success in terms of political bets or electoral support at different moments in its history. The company provided support to a succession of candidates to public office: Frondizi, Viola, the Peronist candidate in 1983 (and in previous years), Ítalo Luder, Chacho Álvarez, Fernando de la Rúa, Duhalde and Macri (with almost militant fervor). They all failed in their administrations or lost the elections. Furthermore, as Sivak documents, *Clarín* kept in touch with the *carapintada* insurgents who rose up against the constitutional tenure of Raúl Alfonsín.

Indeed, the diagnoses of the political situation by the Group's leadership usually proved wrong. Misjudgments in this area multiplied starting in 2009, including repeated predictions decreeing the death of Kirchnerism, which, albeit with reflux, managed to endure as a legitimate option for large sectors of the population, and demonstrated a persistence and social rooting against all forecasts of apocalyptic decline in recent decades. For this reason, the economic instinct of Grupo Clarín's leadership proved to be much better than its political instinct.

In identifying targets to expand activities toward more lucrative businesses, Magnetto recognized the opportunities opened up by other players and competitors in the media market. That was the case in 1984 when the license for free-to-air TV Channel 9 in Buenos Aires was granted to Alejandro Romay, who increased the revenues of the only private station among all other state-run channels. It was also through the experience of others that Grupo Clarín made its foray into the cable TV space in the early 1990s and captured the rights to broadcast soccer league matches. Later on, its entry into the telecommunications arena was inspired by other international experiences and the realization of the scale and cash flow growth that a multimedia conglomerate can reap by being a leading player in converged services. Grupo Clarín first tested models of horizontal concentration, then ventured into vertical and multimedia integration and finally deployed a conglomerate and convergent model. Once it strengthened its initial business with its stake in Papel Prensa – partnering with the state during the dictatorship – the Group gained momentum with practices that were at odds with the principles of competition, in addition to discretionary support from different governments to enter other adjacent industries.

According to Sivak, Grupo Clarín understood where capitalist accumulation was going, and recognized the pro-development background of Magnetto (and before him, Frigerio). Those tools were key for Magnetto to operate in the context of the historical and economic structure of Argentina.

No other businessman in Argentina has taken advantage of convergence as Magnetto has. He even outdid Carlos Slim in Claro and the leadership of Movistar, a Telefónica company, whose starting points were more advantageous than Grupo Clarín's until 2015, both in economic terms (income and investment possibilities) and in the ownership of infrastructure networks as platforms for services. Furthermore, through its influence on Macri's regulatory policy, Clarín blocked any possibility for Claro and Movistar to deploy convergent services. That possibility emerged with the enactment of Telecommunications and ICT Law No. 28078 ("Argentina Digital") in late 2014 and was later on reversed by a Macri decree. Nonetheless, neither Claro nor Movistar took advantage of this window of opportunity for convergence, partly because they were focused on expanding 4G networks under the bidding process for the allocation of spectrum bands in 2014. It is true that the regulatory obstacles faced by Grupo Clarín's competitors conditioned their business, but it is no less true that the Group designed effective plans to eliminate hindrances for itself, while obstacles for the rest of the players in the industries in which it operates persisted.

Grupo Clarín's expansion strategy has been incremental over the last 45 years, but mainly limited to the Argentine market. It would not be fair to say that this strategy shows aversion to risk; however, it has not been daring either, and it may be described as rather moderate. Grupo Clarín only participates in businesses when it has a controlling interest of corporate affairs and management in the companies in which it invests, bolstering its growth with an indebtedness and reinvestment strategy. For Magnetto, there have been two very important constraints to its expansion within, but especially outside, Argentina: The size of the market (which is relatively small when compared to Brazil or Mexico) and the lack of domestic credit. For this reason, the Group resorted to two major foreign indebtedness processes to finance its growth: During the 1990s, it expanded its cable TV business (Multicanal) and became one of the main operators in this lucrative market, and, in 2016, it initiated the Cablevisión-Telecom merger. This funding strategy has been coupled with a generous distribution of dividends to shareholders and an active presence on the Buenos Aires and London stock markets.

Is Clarín a domestic group with its growth confined within the perimeter of the Argentine territory? Will it be able to preserve its dominant position over time in all of the market segments where it operates in Argentina? In other words, will it be able to shield itself (as it has done so far) under the protection of different governments through aids and regulations, faced with radical transformations in the info-communication economy and the threat of global digital platforms as little respectful of state sovereignty (the so-called Clarín "national champion" style)? To maintain its leadership position in all Argentine info-communication segments, Grupo Clarín would need to expand its activities to globalized environments ranging from data storage and processing in the cloud (where Amazon is the main global player) to over-the-top (OTT) video services on demand. In this latter space, the Group developed its Flow offering; however, the exclusive content of Netflix, Disney+, HBO or Amazon Prime at an international level exceeds the capabilities and resources of a conglomerate like Grupo Clarín.

At present, Grupo Clarín is faced with two challenges: One has to do with the structure of the sector and the Group's room for maneuvering; the other pertains to the person whole ads it. Regarding the first challenge, in the digital metamorphosis of the media and telecommunications economy, Grupo Clarín has the privilege of having been the only incumbent with sufficient resources to provide convergent services in recent years, as well as fixed and mobile telecom and ICT networks through the Cablevisión-Telecom merger. While its digital media units have so far been unprofitable, its infrastructure ownership and its leadership in converged products and services place it in a good position. However, the entry of much larger global digital conglomerates with rules of the game not defined by the Argentine State – which was always so responsive to Grupo Clarín – contributes to questions about the ability of Magnetto's group to adapt to or be resilient to this new reality. In one of the books commissioned by the Group, Magnetto states that the current uncertainty and the global scale of the information and communication markets make Google and Facebook "large" players, with his Group logically ranked in a more modest position (see Magnetto, 2016).

As the largest shareholder and CEO of Grupo Clarín, Magnetto has not been an epitome of innovation, as he has not developed disruptive new businesses, as Sivak points out. He has rather been a strategist with increasing expertise in the interpretation and rapid adaptation of Grupo Clarín to the major trends in the evolution of the info-communication industries. But this growth rationale, comprised of the various stages described in this book, seems to find its limits with the global digitization of the sector, as a networked economy with implications in each of its constitutive segments leaves little room for national strategists and even partners from relatively small markets such as Argentina.

The second challenge that Grupo Clarín faces is the generational change of its shareholders and managers. Magnetto was born in July 1944, and Aranda and Pagliaro belong to the same generation. Although Magnetto asserted in one of his interviews, "We have prepared a Group to survive us – me and each of the shareholders," the truth is that the ties of the heirs to each other, such as those uniting Marcela and Felipe Noble Herrera, will lack the cohesion and leadership that Magnetto himself has guaranteed. This could open up a scenario of shareholder fragmentation in a group that until now has been mainly homogeneous.

Furthermore, Magnetto's ability to identify political priorities, management objectives and expansion and consolidation strategies is not susceptible to extrapolation, especially in a context of change and uncertainty. In her book *Sincerely*, Cristina Fernández de Kirchner describes Magnetto as "the most political" of all the business people she came across in her long career as a deputy, senator, president and vice president of Argentina. Although "political actor" is a befitting description for every media outlet (Borrat, 1989) and, by extension, for every media owner or editor-in-chief, Fernández de Kirchner was alluding to Magnetto's distinctive attribute as a primus inter pares, a politician among politicians, one who managed to reap the benefits of doing business with presidents of contrasting ideologies throughout different phases of recent history. Despite the mutual aversion they show for each other, or perhaps because of that aversion, the description made by Magnetto's adversary works as both a compliment and a warning – it points to an infrequent and exceptional quality, the foreseeable absence of which will shape the path of Argentina's largest info-communication group in the years to come.

References

Borrat, Héctor (1989). "El periódico, actor del sistema político," *Análisis No. 12*, Universitat Autónoma de Barcelona, pp. 67–80.

Magnetto, Héctor (2016). *Así lo viví. El poder, los medios y la política en Argentina*. Buenos Aires: Planeta.

Index

Note: **Bold** page numbers refer to tables; *italic* page numbers refer to figures and page numbers followed by "n" denote endnotes.

accumulation model 15
Act No. 26.053 23
Administración Nacional de Seguridad Social (ANSES) 60, 82
AFA *see* Argentine Soccer Association (AFA)
AGEA 48, 71, 73–74
Agosti, Orlando 34
Agreement on Mutual Protection and Promotion of Investments 21
agricultural sector 9, 22
agro-export model 12
agro-export oligarchy 11, 14
Aguad, Oscar 46
Alfonsín, Raúl 37, 50, 69, 104, 130; decline of 38; economic crisis 38; return to democracy 16–21
Alianza Anticomunista Argentina 33
Álvarez, Chacho 130
Amazon Prime Video App 89
ANSES *see* Administración Nacional de Seguridad Social (ANSES)
anti-Kirchnerism 129
anti-Peronism 31
Apold, Raúl 30
Aramburu, Pedro Eugenio 31, 50, 51n2
Aranda, Alma 60
Aranda, Héctor 60, 127, 133
Aranda, José Antonio 57–58, 62, 68, 71
Argentina: acute crisis 113; broadcasting system 15, 17; businessman in 131; cross-media conglomerate in 96; debt with IMF 22; economic instability 8; foreign debt 19; inflationary crisis 17; newspaper in 106; political and economic processes 7; political and economic shifts 128; political and economic spasms 126; right to freedom of expression and eradication of censorship 37; social classes in 123
Argentine Bankruptcy Law 23
Argentine Digital Law 46
Argentine Football Association 20–21
Argentine Revolution 12
Argentine Soccer Association (AFA) 39
Argentine TV system 124n18
Aristotelian concept of "political animal" 49
Ariza, Guillermo 104, 106
Arte Radiotelevisivo Argentino (ARTEAR) 71–73, 80
Audiovisual Communication Services Law 2, 45–47, 81, 119
audiovisual market 20, 39, 40
audiovisual media 20, 35, 38, 44, 110, 112, 129
Audiovisual Services Act No. 26.522 24
Audiovisual Services Law 82

Index

Aulicino, Jorge 106, 107, 111, 114, 116, 117
"Avellaneda Massacre" 41
Ávila, Carlos 39

Bankruptcy Law 113
Bardengo, Sebastián 59, 60
Basualdo, Eduardo 9, 15, 16
Bayer, Osvaldo 99, 102
Bedoian, Juan 115
Borges, Jorge Luis 104, 107
Borrat, Héctor 28, 49
Borrelli, Marcelo 3, 36
Botana, Natalio 29, 98
Brady Plan 18–19
Brazilian Grupo Globo 127
broadband 1, 2, 48; distribution of 89; internet and cable TV services 63; market share of 75; wireless 55
broadcasting and telecommunication services 20
Broadcasting Decree 38
Broadcasting Law 70, 71
broadcasting system: aggregate audiences for 65; Argentina 15, 17
broadcast owners 13
"bureaucratic-authoritarian state" 12
business: growth of 2; lines of 62–67, 79, *79,* 88–90; printing and publishing lines of 80; revenues per business line 86, **87**

cable TV market 18, 39, 40, 54, 63, 72, 79, *79,* 111, 131; Argentine Football Association and Televisión Codificada SA agreement 20–21; distribution of 89; and enactment of Audiovisual Communication Services Law No. 26522 45; nonprofit organizations to provide 23; sustained growth of 80
Cablevisión 2, 23, 40, 42, 43, 54, 55, 63, 67, 72, 73, 129; stake in Multicanal 75; telecommunications merger between Telecom and 46
Cablevisión Holding (CVH) 55–57, 79, 88, 92n25; Board of Directors of 91n2; shareholders *58*; value of share 93n27
Cablevisión-Multicanal merger 75, 78, 80; key in business strategy 77
Cablevisión-Telecom merger 5, 47, 48, 56, 61, 63, 67, 92n26, 128, 132, 133
Cafiero, Antonio 38
Calamaro, Eduardo 102
Camilion, Oscar 32, 33, 51n3
Cámpora, Héctor 12, 26n3, 33
Canal 7 13–14, 43
Canal 13 38, 65, 71, 80, 92n15; privatization of 109–110
Canal Volver 72
capitalism 127
capital-labor struggle 12
Cassino, Damián 60
Cavallo, Domingo 18
CEI-Telefónica 72
censorship: eradication of 37; media system 34
CGT *see* General Labor Confederation (CGT)
Channel 13, license of 20
CIMECO 73
Circulation Verification Institute 118
Cisneros (Venezuela) 128
Citibank 20
Clarín 1–3, 14, 15–16, 28, 51n4, 129; adherence of leadership 34; after Perón's death 33; broadest circulation newspaper 54; building business strategy 130; build-up and expansion process 7; confrontation and metamorphosis (2009–2020) 118–122; consolidation of 109; controversial purchase of Papel Prensa 68; creation of 54; cross-media conglomerate consolidation (1982–2001) 105–112; cultural profile 122; digital media outlets 67; editorial department of 103; evolution of 110; expansion and consolidation of 70; foundations of 30; government's favoritism toward 31; growth strategy 90; largest circulation 65; line of enthusiastic political support 36; media and 8–10; newspaper of urban middle classes 96; Noble era (1945–1969) 97–101; offers subscription TV

service 78; partner in Papel Prensa 37; recovery and national culture (2001–2009) 113–118; relationship between culture and 122; sales of 18; uprising of *carapintada* military insurgents 38
clarin.com 54
Claro 51, 64, 131, 132
Class A Shares 59–60
CMD *see* Compañía de Medios Digitales (CMD)
CNDC *see* Comisión Nacional de Defensa de la Competencia (CNDC)
cohesion: and leadership 128–129; shareholding stability and 128
Comisión Nacional de Defensa de la Competencia (CNDC) 55
commercial broadcasters 14
communication: ecosystem 50; in Latin America 48; public policymaking in 47
Communist Party 102
Compañía de Medios Digitales (CMD) 77
Compañía de Teléfonos del Interior (CTI) 52n10, 71, 73
Confirmado 32
conglomerate 28; cross-media 1, 7, 54, 56, 96; expansion of 50; expansive dynamics of 50; Grupo Clarín and 42, 45; media 72; organizational structure of 40; Telefónica 45, 51
constitutional reform 19, 21, 39
Conti, Haroldo 99
control, dictatorship and media 14–16
corporate structure 54–56; Board of Directors 56; management structure of *61,* 61–62; shareholders 56–61, *58–59, 61*
Cossa, Tito 99
Costa, Flavia 115, 122
coup d'état 8, 12, 14, 30, 32, 34, 103
"crisis of the countryside" 43–44
Crítica 123n1; Culture and Nation supplement 99, 100, 102–104; developmentalism (1969–1982) 101–105; relationship with Frondicism 100; Sports and Entertainment section 99–100
Crónica 32, 34, 37
cross-media conglomerate 1, 7, 54, 56, 96; consolidation (1982–2001) 105–112
cross-media initiative 77
CTI *see* Compañía de Teléfonos del Interior (CTI)
Cuban Revolution 32
Cultural Asset and Heritage Preservation Law 92n20
cultural journalism 96–97
cultural products, impact on 121
Culture and Nation supplement, *Crítica* 99, 100, 102–104
CVH *see* Cablevisión Holding (CVH)
Cytrynblum, Marcos 103, 104, 106, 107, 112

D'Ambrosio, Martín 60
defensive concentration process (2002–2008) 41–43
deindustrialization process 14
De la Rúa, Fernando 130; return to democracy 16–21
democracy: and multimedia expansion (1983–2002) 37–41; return to 16–21
Democratic Union 29
developmentalism 49, 101–105
developmentalists 105, 106, 122
dictatorship 18, 31, 32, 69; and deals (1976–1983) 34–37; and IMF and foreign banks programs 22; and media 14–16
digital convergence 4, 67, 89, 90
digital restructuring 88–90
digitization 2, 5; changes and challenge of 121; of cultural markets 97; development of 77; of Grupo Clarín's cable networks and media 54; impact on media offer 119; and platformization 46
Dillon, Alfredo 116–117
direct communication 43
DirecTV 63, 72, 73
dividends: payment of 82, **83**; to shareholders 80, *81,* 82
documentary sources 1

138 *Index*

Duhalde, Eduardo 20–22, 41, 130
Durruty, Enrique 33
DyN News Agency 37, 69

Economic Commission for Latin America and the Caribbean (ECLAC) 11
economic crisis 13, 19, 74
economic disorders 127
economic policies 14–16
Ejército Revolucionario del Pueblo 33
El Mundo 68
ENaCom 48
Entel 20
Ente Nacional de Comunicaciones (ENACOM) 55
equity: and Board composition 60; in Papel Prensa and *Radio Mitre* 71
Etchevers, Martín 74, 77, 88
Eurnekian, Eduardo 92n19

Farrell, Edelmiro 8
Fernández, Alberto 26, 40, 42, 45, 47
Fernández de Kirchner, Cristina 2, 5, 21, 23–25, 28, 42, 79–80, 82, 92n24, 96, 97, 103, 119; *Sincerely* 133; war against (2008–2015) 43–45
Fibertel 61, 75
Film Law (1994) 42
financial sector: and privatized public services companies 22; reform of 15
financial value 17, 18
Fintech Advisory 55, 59
"First Peronism" 9
FM 100 37, 39
Folha de Sao Paulo 127
Fontanarrosa, Roberto 116
Ford, Aníbal 106, 108
foreign capital 13, 19–21; in media ownership 39
foreign debt 22
Foreign Direct Investment (FDI) 21
"free market" 18
free-to-air 112; TV Channel 9 131; TV network 39–40; TV space 65, 71
FREJULI 12
Fresco, Manuel 29
Frigerio, Octavio 33

Frigerio, Rogelio 5, 31, 32–33, 36, 97, 100–104, 123n7
Frigerism 101–102; detachment from 106; and economic efficiency criteria 105; influence of 103
Frondizi, Arturo 11, 30–32, 51n2, 68, 100, 123n7, 130; administration 11–12
Frondizi-Frigerio style developmentalism 36
Frondizi-Frigerism movement 100
Fund for the Development of Pulp and Paper Production (1969) 51n4
Fútbol para Todos program 45, 52n9

García, Héctor Ricardo 29, 32, 52n7, 99
Gardel, Carlos 115
GC *see* Grupo Clarín (GC)
Gelbard, José Ber 33, 68
General Labor Confederation (CGT) 30
Gerchunoff, Pablo 9, 14
German Embassy 29
Global Media Giants (GMG) series 1
Goldman Sachs 57, 78
Gómez, Albino 103
González, Baruki Luis 60
González, Horacio 100, 102, 117–118
Graiver, David 35, 51n4
Grinspun, Bernardo 17
Grupo Clarín (GC) 1, 7–8, 55; academic and journalistic studies on 122; administration's media policies 26; Board of Directors of 91n2; business model and income structure of 130; cash flow 128; challenges of 133; consolidation process of 3; cultural project 5; cultural services 96; development of 3; economic profile 5; editorial line management 130; evolution of share *81*; expansion strategy 132; "the first Argentine holding of converged communications," 84–88, *85, 86,* **87**; first phase of expansion 70, *70*; fourth phase of expansion 84–85, *85*; growth of 2; history of 56, 127; license of Channel 13 20; limits imposed

on media ownership 25; lines of business, evolution of 79, *79*; management structure of *61*, 61–62; participation in forums and press associations 126–127; political and economic spasms 126; political dimension 4; politics (*see* politics, Grupo Clarín); revenues per business line 86, **87**; second phase of expansion 75–76, *76*; self-congratulatory statement 98–99; seventy-five years of 90–91; stages in evolution 128–129; strength of 2; structure of *57*; tensions between government and 17
Grupo Globo 4, 62, 127
Grupo Graiver 68
Guareschi, Roberto 106, 107, 111, 112

Harrison, Carlos 60
Herrera, Felipe Noble 57, 60, 62, 127, 133
Herrera, Marcela Noble 57, 59, 62, 127, 133
Hita, Gonzalo 61
Hora, Roy 97, 98
Humor 102

Ibáñez, Mariano 60
Illia, Arturo 12, 30, 32, 50
"independent journalism" 44
Independent Socialist Party 28
industrialization 9, 10
inflation 17, 18, 24
information-communication groups 127
Initial Public Offering (IPO) 55
"institutional instability" 47
integration process: monomedia expansion (1945–1988) 67–71, **70**, *70*; multimedia expansion (1989–2006) 70–88, *76, 79, 81,* **83,** *85, 86,* **87**; stages of 67
Intellectual Property Law No. 11723 28–29
Inter-American Commission on Human Rights 47
Inter-American Court of Human Rights 45

international credit 19, 25
internationalization 128
internet segment 79, *79*
internet services 55, 80, 84

Jauretche, Arturo 100
JP Morgan & Co. 20
Justicialist Party 19

Kirchnerism 21–25, 40, 111, 119, 120, 122, 129, 131; and Grupo Clarín relationship 43–45
Kirchner, Néstor 21–25, 41–44, 47, 50, 74, 129
Kirschbaum, Ricardo 114, 115

La Nación 16, 29, 30, 34, 35, 51n4, 67–69
Lanata, Jorge 29, 51n4
Landi, Oscar 108
Lanusse, Alejandro 12, 68
La Opinion 34
La Prensa 13, 30, 34, 68
La Razón 16, 34, 35, 51n4, 67, 69
Lastiri, Raúl 14, 26n3
Latin America 127; communications in 48; media groups in 7; unionization 9
Lavieri, Omar 106, 108, 110
La Voz del Interior 65
Law for the Preservation of Cultural Assets and Heritage 23, 41, 113
Levín, Florencia 3
Levingston, Roberto 12
"Liberating Revolution" (1955–1958) 31
lines of business 62–67, 88–90
Llach, Lucas 9, 14
López, José Ignacio 105
Los Andes 65
Luciani, Luca 60
Luder, Ítalo 37, 130
Luna, Félix 99

Macri, Mauricio 2–3, 25, 26, 40, 45, 46, 50, 60, 128–130; media market in 49; public policymaking in communications 47; regulations to needs of *Clarín*'s shareholders 48
Macrism 25

magazine: *Humor* 102; market segments *64*, 65; *Ñ* 113–118, 121, 122; *Qué* 100, 102
Magnetto, Héctor 3, 4, 8, 33, 36–38, 43, 50, 55–57, 62, 68, 69, 71, 105, 109, 113, 120, 121, 127, 128, 131–134
Magnetto, Horacio 60
Magnetto, Marcia 60
Malvinas/Falklands War (1982) 34
market segments: newspaper and magazine *64*, 65; press and radio 64, *64*
market share 62–67; aggregate audiences AM-FM radio stations *66*; fixed broadband *63*; mobile lines *64*; pay TV *64*; programming channels *66*
Márquez, Gabriel García 104
Martínez, David 55, 60, 91n7, 91n11, 92n24
Martínez de Hoz, José 14
Marxist groups 12
Massera, Emilio 34
media: and *Clarín* 8–10; and communications groups 41; concentration of 18, 21, 23–25; dictatorship and 14–16; in general and audiovisual sector 43; heritage of fertileculture 40; and information-communication groups 127; in Latin America 7; political economy of 3; technological changes in 4; and telecommunications economy 133
media conglomerates 42, 45, 62, 71, 72, 126
media market 41, 62, 120, 131
media policies 10, 13, 17, 20–26, 43, 45, 71
mega-merger rules 46–51
Menem, Carlos 7–8, 38, 39, 41, 42, 50, 71, 72; return to democracy 16–21
"militant journalism" 44
military dictatorship 12, 14, 103
Military Junta 15, 34, 36; trial of 37
"military party" 11
Mitre, Bartolomé 29
mobile communications 2, 64, 86

Mochkofsky, Graciela 3, 35, 51n5, 108
Molinas, Ricardo 35
Moltini, Carlos 60–61, 90
monomedia expansion, integration process 67–71, **70**, *70*
Montoneros 68
Movistar 131, 132
Multicanal 23, 39, 40, 42, 43, 55, 67, 73, 129; cable TV with the purchase of 72; Cablevisión stake in 75; debt 73
multimedia: expansion, integration process (1989–2006) 70–88, *76*, *79*, *81*, **83**, *85*, *86*, **87**; expansion of 37–41; expansion stage 67; process of expansion 55

Ñ 121, 122; balance between national and international contents 117; culture for 115; editing of 118; emergence of 116; launch of 113–114; representative of cultural profile evolution 118; writing staff of 116
Nación, Banco 31
national culture, conference on 101
National Development Bank 16, 69
"National Reorganization Process" 14
Necessity and Urgency Decree No. 267/15 47
Necessity and Urgency Decree No. 527/05 23
Neustadt, Bernardo 99
newspaper 15; and cable services 73; *Clarín* (*see Clarín*); *Crónica* 32; culture section of 96–97; disappearance of 127; *El Mundo* 68; foundation of 29; impact on sales 109; *La Nación* 16, 67; *La Prensa* 13; *La Razón* 16, 67; *La Voz del Interior* 65; leadership of 35, 36; *Los Andes* 65; market segments *64*, 65; mass scale of 32; motto of 51n1; sales of 18, *70*
newsprint paper 10, 16, 26n2
Nextel 2, 46, 48; acquisition of 54, 79; revenue from 86

Noble, Ernestina Herrera de 3, 4, 31, 36, 51n5, 62, 71, 101, 104
de Noble, Herrera 32
Noble, Roberto 1, 28, 29, 31, 49, 60, 62, 68, 69, 97, 127, 128; 1945–1969 97–101; conception of culture 102; economic policy 30; succession of 33

O'Donnell, Guillermo 12
Olé 110
Onganía, Juan Carlos 12, 32, 51n4
online video streaming service, development of 89
Oropeza, Mariano 117, 118
Ortiz, Raúl Scalabrini 100
over-the-top (OTT) video services 132–133

Página 12 44, 108, 111
Pagliaro, Francisco 60
Pagliaro, Lucio Rafael 57, 62, 68, 71, 88, 127, 133
Papaleo, Lidia 35
Papel Prensa 2, 16, 35, 73, 103, 131; acquisition of 69; case of 45; *Clarín* partner in 37; controversial purchase of 68; equity in 71; origin of 51n4
Patino, Roxana 107
Pavón, Héctor 116–119, 121
pay TV 112; consumption of 120; service of 78; stations 92n15, 92n16
Paz, José C. 29
Perez Companc 20
Peronism 18, 25, 26, 106; banning of 32; electoral ban on 33; fall of 100; media and *Clarín,* (1945–1955) 8–13; multi-class ranks of 129; proposal of 20; referents aligned behind renovated agenda 38; return to power 14
Peronist movement 12
Peronist Youth 12
peronization 12
Perón, Juan Domingo 8, 11, 26n3, 29, 30, 100, 103, 123n2; death of 33; second mandate 12
Perón, María Estela Martínez de 12, 30

Personal (Telecom) 86
Pichon-Riviere, Enrique 106
Pichon-Riviere, Marcelo 106
Poliladron 124n19
political developments 28
political-electoral expressions 130
political journalism 29
political sectors 129
political unrest, cycle of 10–14
politics, Grupo Clarín: defensive concentration (2002–2008) 41–43; democracy and multimedia expansion (1983–2002) 37–41; developmentalist platform (1958–1976) 31–34; dictatorship and deals (1976–1983) 34–37; mega-merger and tailor-made rules (2015–2020) 46–51; wake-up call (1945–1958) 28–31; war against CFK (2008–2015) 43–45
Portantiero, Juan Carlos 11, 99
Prebisch, Raúl 11
presidential reelection 26n1
press, aggregate audiences for 65
PRIMA 72; shares of 75
Primera Plana 32
private media 15, 23, 35, 36; partnership between dictatorial state and 35
private TV 13–14, 32
privatization 18, 38; control and 14–16; of public companies 18; of telecommunications sector 20; of TV channels 20
public censorship 33
public debt, issuance of 19
public funds, management of 29

Qué 100, 102
Quiero Música 92n15
Quintana, Hamlet Lima 99

Radical Civic Union (UCR) 12, 16, 19
Radical Civic Union Party (UCRI) 32, 38, 51n2, 100
radicalism 10, 17–18
radicalization 12
Radio 10 109
Radio La 100 66

radio market 66
Radio Mitre 37, 39, 66, 109; acquisition of 70; equity in 71
Ramos, Julio 3, 29, 99
Rébori, Blanca 99, 102
Rendo, Jorge 60
repression: combination of 34; state repression mechanisms 33
Revolución Libertadora 68
Rincón, Omar 43
Rivera, Jorge 96, 106
Romay, Alejandro 131
de la Rúa, Fernando 40

Sábato, Ernesto 100, 104
Santo Domingo (Colombia) 128
self-censorship 15, 104
Serrat, Joan Manuel 104
shareholders: Cablevisión Holding 58; dividends to *81*, 82; presence and influence of 59; structure of Telecom Argentina 59, *59*
shareholding stability 128
Sincerely (Fernández de Kirchner) 133
Sivak, Martín 3, 29, 30, 43, 71, 98–100, 104–106, 108, 119, 121, 130, 131, 133
Slim, Carlos 131
socialism 10
sociedad anónima 55, 73
Sofovich, Bernardo 33
Spanish-language newspaper 104
State Reform Law 20, 38
Supercanal 63

tailor-made rules 46–51
Tax Authority (AFIP) 44
Techint 20
technology transformations 128
Telecentro 63
Telecom Argentina 2, 44, 54, 56, 57, 78, 92n14; authorization to purchase shares in 60; composition of 60; management structure of *61*, 61–62; shareholder structure of 59, *59*; telecommunications merger between Cablevisión and 46
telecommunications 131; and audiovisual sectors 21; merger between Cablevisión and Telecom 46; privatization of 20
Telecommunications and ICT Law No. 28078 132
telecom networks 90–91
Telefé 39, 65, 92n16
Telefónica Argentina 20, 39, 40, 45, 51, 63, 74
Telefónica España 20
Televisa 3, 4, 127
Televisión Codificada SA 20–21
Televisión Satelital Codificada (TSC) company 52n9
Timerman, Jacobo 29, 32, 99
Todo Noticias (TN) 72
Tuñón, Raúl González 99

UCR *see* Radical Civic Union (UCR)
UCRI *see* Radical Civic Union Party (UCRI)
United States: Agreement on Mutual Protection and Promotion of Investments with 21; television networks of 13
Urricelqui, Alejandro 60

Valiente, Ignacio Sáenz 59
Verbitsky, Horacio 44
Verdaguer, Hernán 61
Verón, Eliseo 108, 129
Viacom 65
Vico, Juan Martín 61
Vidal, Germán 59
Videla, Jorge 20, 34, 35, 52n7, 103; Broadcasting Decree-Law 21
Video Cable Comunicación (VCC) 72
Viola, Roberto 130

Walsh, María Elena 104
war journalism 49, 50, 129

Zaffore, Carlos 33
Zona 111
zoon politikon 49–51